Table of Contents

Introduction

Do you want your child to be
focused, reliable, and energetic?

Do you want your child to be
self-motivated and make good decisions?

Do you want your child to have
stable moods and good mental health?

Do you want your child to be
able to handle everyday stress?

Do you want your child to
perform well academically?

Do you want your child to
get along with others?

Do you want your child to
**grow up to be an independent
young adult?**

Of course, you do! I know I did with my daughter Chloe. Like most parents, I wanted to provide her with the tools necessary to help her have the best life possible. And I have to admit, that selfishly, I wanted to make parenting easier for me in the process. One of the best ways to help kids develop a healthy brain and mental fortitude is through good food choices. Here's the secret: It all starts with you! The foods you have in your home and the meals you prepare for your kids play a vital role in their physical and mental well-being.

Published by MindWorks Press, Newport Beach, California
A Division of Amen Clinics, Inc.
www.amenclinics.com
Authors: Tana Amen, B.S.N., R.N.

Other Books by Tana Amen:

Relentless Courage of a Scared Child
Nelson Books, 2021

The Brain Warrior's Way
Berkley, 2016

The Brain Warrior's Way Cookbook
Berkley, 2016

Healing ADD Through Food
MindWorks Press, 2014

The Omni Diet
New York Times Bestseller, St. Martin's Griffin, 2013

Eat Healthy With the Brain Doctor's Wife Cookbook
MindWorks Press, 2011

Get Healthy With the Brain Doctor's Wife Coaching Guide
MindWorks Press, 2011

Change Your Brain, Change Your Body Cookbook
MindWorks Press, 2011

If your kids eat a junk-food diet, then they'll have a junk-food brain and mindset. It will drain their energy, zap their motivation and focus, and increase stress and anxiousness. A poor diet will also make it harder for them to stick with the family rules and can contribute to irritability, aggression, defiance, and more. This can lead to family strife, which makes parenting so much more challenging.

Give them nutrient-dense, healthy foods, however, and they'll have a better brain, a better outlook, and a better life. Fueling the brain with nutritious food will help increase focus and energy, balance moods, calm anxiousness, improve academic performance, enhance sociability, and strengthen resilience to stress. This contributes to a happier family life and fewer parenting struggles.

I'll let you in on a little secret when it comes to cooking. In a perfect world I would make every meal from scratch. But it isn't a perfect world. I'm a busy parent—and I know you're busy too—so I do the best I can. When I'm in a rush I cut corners on recipes by purchasing pre-chopped onion, peeled garlic, pre-cooked free-range rotisserie chicken, and other time-savers. It's still better than ordering food or eating out. Simply do the best you can and get your kids involved in the process. Get them thinking about the foods they eat and encourage them to participate in grocery shopping, meal planning, and cooking. Most of all, make it fun!

Cooking together is a great bonding experience that creates lasting memories. This cookbook will help you get started. I can assure you that all the delicious recipes in this cookbook are completely brain healthy and 100% kid-tested. Even better, some of the recipes are so simple kids can make them on their own. Let's get cooking!

Tana Amen

EASY BREEZY SIPS

Lemon Slush

Serves 2

Ingredients:

16-20 ounces cold sparkling water

1 lemon, squeezed

Handful of ice

2 droppers full of liquid stevia (lemon flavor)

Preparation:

1. Add all ingredients to blender bowl (preferably high-powered blender).

2. Turn blender on low at first, then increase speed for about 30 seconds.

3. Add additional water or ice as needed to achieve desired consistency.

4. Pour into two large glasses and serve cold.

Brain Healthy Hot Chocolate

Serves 2

Ingredients:

1 teaspoon organic raw cocoa powder

16 ounces organic, unsweetened, vanilla-flavored almond milk

2 droppers full of liquid stevia (I prefer chocolate flavor)

1 tablespoon Rapturous Coconut Whipped Cream
  (see recipe in Sauces and Toppings) or 1 squirt of almond milk
  (non-dairy) whipped cream

Preparation:

1. Heat almond milk to desired temperature.

2. Stir in cocoa powder until it is fully dissolved.

3. Add chocolate-flavored stevia.

4. Top with a swirl of whipped cream.

Spa Water

Serves 2

Ingredients:

16-20 ounces cold sparkling water

Handful of berries (blueberries, strawberries, blackberries)

2 sprigs mint or 2 slices lemon, orange, peach, or melon

Preparation:

1. Pour water into 2 large glasses.

2. Add berries to each glass.

3. Garnish with mint sprigs or fruit slices and serve cold.

Sparkling "Soda"

Serves 2

Ingredients:

16-20 ounces cold sparkling water

2 droppers full of liquid stevia (I prefer orange or chocolate flavor)

Preparation:

1. Pour water into 2 large glasses.

2. Add stevia to each glass and serve cold.

Smoothies

Tana's Tips for Smoothies:

On all smoothie recipes, feel free to add any or all of the following:

Note: One of the best ways to sneak healthy veggies into your child's diet is by adding powdered varieties to their smoothies. Chances are they won't even taste it!

1 scoop freeze-dried greens
   (I use Neuro Greens by BrainMD at BrainMD.com)
1 scoop mushroom powder
   (I use Smart Mushrooms by BrainMD at BrainMD.com)
1 tablespoon flax, hemp, or chia seeds
1 tablespoon fiber (inulin or glucomannan)

Only for the adventurous (try adding one or two of the following for fun):

1 teaspoon maca powder

1 teaspoon pomegranate powder

1 teaspoon acai powder

1 teaspoon camu camu powder

1 teaspoon bee pollen

1 tablespoon aloe gel

Preparation for all smoothies:

1. Add all ingredients to blender bowl
   (preferably high-powered blender).
2. Turn blender on low at first, then increase speed
   for about 30 seconds.
3. Add additional water or ice as needed to
   achieve desired consistency.
4. Pour into two large glasses and serve cold.

Antiox Brain-Boosting Smoothie

Serves 2

Ingredients:

½ cup frozen or fresh pomegranate
    seeds

½ cup frozen organic blueberries

16-20 ounces cold water (or
    unsweetened almond milk);

I prefer water to hydrate first thing
in the morning

Handful of ice

2 cups baby spinach

2 kale leaves, torn from stem
    (or ½ cucumber, sliced)

2 scoops vanilla- or chocolate
    -flavored protein powder
    (pea protein, sweetened with
    stevia; I use Omni Protein
    by BrainMD at BrainMD.com)

2 droppers full of liquid stevia
    (I prefer berry or chocolate flavor)

2 tablespoons coconut butter

Apple Spice Smoothie

Serves 2

Ingredients:

1 large apple

16-20 ounces cold water
    (or unsweetened almond milk);
I prefer water to hydrate first thing
in the morning.

Handful of ice

2 cups baby spinach

1 chard leaf (or 2 kale leaves)
    torn from stem

2 scoops vanilla- or chocolate
    flavored protein powder (pea
    protein, sweetened with stevia;
    I use Omni Protein by BrainMD
    at BrainMD.com)

1 ½ teaspoon pumpkin pie spice
    (premixed spice blend) or use
    the following 3:

    1 teaspoon cinnamon

    ¼ teaspoon ground cloves

    ¼ teaspoon ground nutmeg

2 droppers full of vanilla
    creme-flavored liquid stevia

2 tablespoons avocado butter
    or coconut butter

Berry Clear Morning Smoothie

Serves 2

Ingredients:

½ cup frozen organic blueberries

½ cup frozen organic blackberries

16-20 ounces cold water
(or unsweetened almond milk);

I prefer water to hydrate first thing
in the morning

Handful of ice

2 cups baby spinach

1 chard leaf (or 2 kale leaves)
torn from stem

2 scoops vanilla- or chocolate-flavored
protein powder (pea protein,
sweetened with stevia; I use Omni
Protein by BrainMD at BrainMD.com)

2 droppers full of liquid stevia
(I prefer berry or chocolate flavor)

2 tablespoons coconut butter

Chocolate Macadamia Madness Smoothie

Serves 2

Ingredients:

1 slightly green banana (I like to peel
them, cut them in half, and freeze
in advance)

8 ounces unsweetened almond
milk or water

12-16 ounces cold water
(depending on desired consistency)

Handful of ice

½ cup macadamia nuts

2 cups baby spinach

1 chard leaf (or 2 kale leaves)
torn from stem

2 scoops chocolate-flavored protein
powder (pea protein, sweetened with
stevia; I use Omni Protein by BrainMD
at BrainMD.com)

2 droppers full of liquid stevia
(I prefer berry or chocolate flavor)

1 tablespoon raw cacao powder
(optional)

Peaches and Cream Smoothie

Serves 2

Ingredients:

1 cup frozen organic peaches

10-12 ounces cold water

8 ounces unsweetened almond milk

Handful of ice

2 cups baby spinach

2 kale leaves, torn from stem
(or 1 small cucumber, sliced)

2 scoops vanilla- or chocolate-flavored
protein powder (pea protein,
sweetened with stevia; I use Omni
Protein by BrainMD at BrainMD.com)

2 droppers full of liquid stevia
(I prefer berry or chocolate flavor)

2 tablespoons coconut butter

Focus and Energy Smoothie

Serves 2

Ingredients:

½ cup frozen organic raspberries

½ cup frozen organic blackberries

16-20 ounces iced green tea

Handful of ice

2 cups baby spinach

2 kale leaves, torn from stem

2 scoops vanilla- or chocolate
flavored protein powder (pea protein,
sweetened with stevia; I use Omni
Protein by BrainMD at BrainMD.com)

2 droppers full of liquid stevia
(I prefer berry or chocolate flavor)

2 tablespoons avocado
(about ¼ avocado)

Strawberry Mint Cooler Smoothie

Serves 2

Ingredients:

1 cup frozen organic strawberries

2 cups cold water (or unsweetened almond milk); I prefer water to hydrate first thing in the morning

Handful of ice

2 cups baby spinach

4-5 fresh mint leaves

2 kale leaves, torn from stem

2 scoops vanilla- or chocolate-flavored protein powder (pea protein, sweetened with stevia; I use Omni Protein by BrainMD at BrainMD.com)

2 droppers full of liquid stevia (I prefer berry or chocolate flavor)

2 tablespoons coconut butter

Tropical Storm Smoothie

Serves 2

Ingredients:

½ cup frozen organic pineapple

½ cup frozen organic mango

16-20 ounces cold water or, for a creamy piña colada taste, use unsweetened almond milk

Handful of ice

2 cups baby spinach

2 kale leaves, torn from stem

2 scoops vanilla- or chocolate-flavored protein powder (pea protein, sweetened with stevia; I use Omni Protein by BrainMD at BrainMD.com)

2 droppers full of liquid stevia I prefer vanilla creme or mango)

2 tablespoons coconut butter

Breakfast

Foods

Brainy Breakfast Burrito

In the Amen household, we typically "go green" when we eat burritos. That means we use romaine lettuce leaves as a wrap to increase veggie intake and cut calories. If you prefer a tortilla, try coconut wraps (Pure Wraps) or Raw Vegan Flat Bread (WrawP). These can be found in most health food stores or online.

Serves 1

Ingredients:

2 eggs

1 teaspoon coconut butter
or raw organic butter

½ small onion or 1 leek, thinly
sliced (white part only)

1 garlic clove, minced

¼ cup red bell pepper, chopped

¼ cup mushrooms, sliced
(I like crimini or button)

¼ cup broccoli florets, chopped

¼ avocado, sliced

1 tablespoon salsa with no added
sugar

Romaine or iceberg lettuce leaves
or 1 wrap (coconut curry flavor
by Pure Wraps or Raw Vegan
Flat Bread by WrawP)

Preparation:

1. In small bowl, whisk eggs.

2. In medium skillet, heat butter over
medium heat.

3. Add onion or leek and garlic; sauté
for 1 minute.

4. Add bell peppers, mushrooms,
and broccoli; cook 2 to 3 minutes.

5. Add eggs; stir until cooked through.

6. Double up romaine leaves and
spread with salsa as desired and top
with avocado. Put egg mixture in
romaine lettuce leaves and wrap
them up.

7. If using a wrap, heat on skillet over
medium heat for 10 seconds; do
not overcook. Spread each wrap
with 1 tablespoon of salsa and
half of egg mixture; top with
sliced avocado. Roll up and
serve immediately.

Cheesy Chipotle Scramble

Serves 2

Ingredients:

4 eggs

2 teaspoons ghee or grapeseed oil

1 tablespoon fresh herbs
  or 1 teaspoon dried of choice
  (optional)

2-3 tablespoons Raw Chipotle Nut
  Cheese (see recipe in Sauces
  and Toppings)

Salt and pepper to taste

Preparation:

1. Whisk eggs in medium bowl.

2. Heat ghee or oil in skillet over
   medium heat. Add eggs
   and scramble.

3. Add herbs, salt, and pepper.
   Continue scrambling until
   eggs are firm.

4. Just before removing from heat,
   sprinkle in Raw Chipotle Nut
   Cheese so you can blend it.
   Remove from heat immediately
   and serve hot.

Crustless Quiche for Clarity

Try using your favorite vegetables in this quiche. It works great with a variety of herbs and vegetables, including tiny broccoli or cauliflower florets and zucchini.

Serves 6-8

Ingredients:

1 10-ounce box frozen spinach (thawed) or 3 cups fresh spinach, sautéed for several minutes

½ onion, peeled and finely diced

1 carrot, peeled and shredded

1 teaspoon dried rosemary

1 teaspoon dried thyme

1 teaspoon sea salt (optional)

12 eggs

1 tablespoon ghee or refined coconut oil

8 ounces ground turkey, chicken, or bison (optional)

1 teaspoon ghee or coconut oil for greasing baking dish

Preparation:

1. Preheat oven to 375° F.

2. If adding ground meat, heat ghee or oil in skillet over medium heat. Add turkey, chicken, or bison until lightly browned but not cooked through.

3. Remove ground meat from skillet and allow to cool for several minutes.

4. Mix spinach, onion, carrot, salt, and herbs in large bowl.

5. Whisk eggs in separate bowl, then add to vegetable and herb blend; mix well.

6. Add ground meat to egg and vegetable mixture.

7. Pour egg mixture into greased 9 x 9-inch baking pan and bake for about 45 minutes until golden brown and fluffy. (It's normal for quiche to deflate when removed from the oven.)

8. Cut into squares and serve hot.

Great Brain Granola

To increase protein and nutritional value, place nuts and seeds in a large bowl, cover with water and soak overnight to initiate sprouting process.

Serves 4

Ingredients:

2 cups slivered almonds

½ cup macadamia nuts, chopped

½ cup cashews, chopped

½ cup pumpkin seeds

½ cup sunflower seeds

¼ cup goji berries or ¼ cup dates, chopped

¼ cup raisins

½ teaspoon vanilla extract

½ teaspoon cinnamon

½ teaspoon sea salt

2 cups almond, coconut, or hemp milk

2 cups plain coconut milk yogurt

¼ cup cacao nibs or ¼ cup Lily's sugar-free dark chocolate chips (optional)

Preparation:

1. If you soaked the nuts and seeds, drain and rinse them, discarding the soaking water.

2. Add nuts, seeds, goji berries or dates, and raisins to food processor and pulse a few times until coarsely chopped to the consistency of granola (do not over-process). Add vanilla, cinnamon, and sea salt to mixture and pulse briefly to incorporate all ingredients.

3. If desired, warm in oven at 175° F for 15 minutes.

4. Divide granola evenly among four bowls.

5. Pour ½ cup almond, coconut, or hemp milk into each bowl of granola.

6. Top each bowl with ½ cup coconut yogurt and add optional toppings as desired.

Omni-Style Crepes

Serves 4

Topping Ingredients:

1 cup fresh organic strawberries, stems removed

½ cup full-fat coconut milk from can refrigerated overnight (skim cream from top after refrigerated) (optional)

1 ½ tablespoons monk fruit (optional)

2 teaspoons ground cinnamon (optional)

1 cup fresh organic blueberries

2 tablespoons unsweetened carob chips (optional)

Batter Ingredients:

½ cup almond meal or coconut flour

½ cup all-purpose gluten-free flour

2 tablespoons flaxseed meal

1 ½ tablespoons monk fruit

1 teaspoon baking powder

5 egg whites

1 cup plain unsweetened almond milk or rice milk

1 teaspoon pure vanilla extract

Topping Preparation:

1. Put strawberries in a high-powered blender. If desired, add coconut milk to blender. Puree until strawberries become a smooth sauce.

Pour sauce into a squeeze bottle (cake decorator), or just pour into a dish, cover, and set aside.

2. If desired, mix monk fruit and cinnamon to sprinkle later.

Crepes Preparation:

1. In large mixing bowl, combine dry ingredients: almond meal or coconut flour, gluten-free flour, flaxseed meal, monk fruit, and baking powder.

2. Add egg whites, almond milk or rice milk, and vanilla. Using a whisk or handheld electric mixer at medium speed, beat batter until smooth. Do not allow batter to rest for long, as the flax tends to thicken it. For best results, the batter should be thin.

3. Use a non-Teflon nonstick crepe pan or small skillet over medium heat. Pour a little less than ¼ cup of batter into pan (just enough to cover the pan with a thin layer), tilting the pan with a circular motion so the batter coats the pan evenly. Cook the pancake for about 1 minute until the bottom is golden brown. Loosen with a spatula, turn over and cook the other side for about 30 seconds. Use your hand to help flip it if necessary. Remove the crepe and set aside on a plate, then repeat with the remaining batter.

4. Place crepe on a plate for serving and put a line of blueberries down the center. You may choose to put a dollop of the strawberry sauce down the center as well, reserving enough of the sauce to garnish the top later. Roll the crepe. Repeat with all the remaining crepes.

5. When the crepes are assembled, place them back in the pan, four or five at a time, for about 30 seconds on each side. When thoroughly warmed, remove and place two to a plate; decorate the top of each plate with a generous serving of the strawberry sauce. Squeeze bottles lend themselves to great designs that kids love. You can also let kids use the squeeze bottle to create their own designs. Otherwise, spoon about a tablespoon over each crepe.

6. If desired, sprinkle 4 or 5 carob chips across the top of each crepe. Kids love this! It gives the illusion of decadence.

7. Sprinkle a generous amount of cinnamon-monk fruit mixture across the entire plate. Serve warm.

Notes: Crepes made with almond meal and gluten-free flour are heavier and a little trickier to turn. If you have trouble, try using a little nonstick spray in your skillet. These crepes are worth the effort. They taste great and are much healthier than regular crepes! Stack the crepes on a plate as you finish them. As you get better at making them, you may choose to make two at a time. Use parchment paper between crepes to prevent sticking and to keep warm, or quickly reheat them before serving.

Pesto Egg Burrito

Serves 2

Ingredients:

1 tablespoon coconut oil

4 eggs

2 tablespoons pesto (see below)

2 coconut wraps

Pesto Ingredients:

1 bunch cilantro

½ cup macadamia nuts

2 cloves garlic

¼ teaspoon sea salt

½ cup macadamia nut oil

Pesto preparation:

1. Blend all ingredients in a food processor until smooth.

Burrito Preparation:

1. Melt coconut oil in small skillet over medium heat.

2. Whisk eggs in small bowl until blended.

3. Pour eggs into heated skillet and gently scramble for 2 minutes.

4. Just before removing eggs from skillet, mix in pesto. Do not cook pesto sauce for long.

5. Divide eggs evenly between two coconut wraps. Roll up wraps, tucking bottom so the egg doesn't fall out.

Notes: Try wrapping burrito in parchment paper to help hold it together. If you heat the coconut wraps, be sure not to overheat them. They melt and fall apart quickly. Usually adding the warm eggs to the wrap is enough to warm it. If you decide to warm it, simply lay it in a warm skillet for about 10 seconds and remove.

Power Breakfast Porridge

Serves 4

Ingredients:

2 ripe bananas, mashed

1-2 cups light coconut milk

1 cup water (optional)

½ cup hazelnut flour or almond flour

¼ cup flax meal

¼ cup almond butter

½ teaspoon vanilla extract

1 tablespoon pumpkin pie spice (premixed spice blend) or use the following three:

- 1 teaspoon cinnamon
- ⅛ teaspoon ground cloves
- ⅛ teaspoon ground nutmeg

2 tablespoons raw cacao powder for chocolate flavor (optional)

2 tablespoons pure maple syrup (optional)

2 scoops vanilla- or chocolate-flavored protein powder (pea protein, sweetened with stevia; I use Omni Protein by BrainMD at BrainMD.com)

Optional Toppings:

2 tablespoons golden raisins

2 tablespoons shredded coconut

2 tablespoons sugar-free dark chocolate chips (Lily's brand)

Preparation:

1. Starting with 1 cup of coconut milk, combine all ingredients except protein powder in medium saucepan and heat to a slow simmer, stirring, until thick and bubbly.

2. Stir in protein powder during the last minute of cooking. Add up to 1 cup of coconut milk or water to blend in protein powder and create desired consistency.

3. Divide evenly into four bowls and sprinkle with your favorite toppings and serve warm.

Simple Pumpkin Pleasure Pancakes

Serves 2

Ingredients:

3 eggs

½ cup organic canned pumpkin

1 teaspoon almond butter

1 teaspoon coconut oil plus more for greasing pan

2 tablespoons flax meal (you can either buy flax meal
at the store or grind whole flax seeds in a coffee grinder)

1 teaspoon pumpkin pie spice

1 teaspoon arrowroot

1 teaspoon coconut sugar or maple syrup (optional)

1 tablespoon Rapturous Coconut Whipped Cream
(optional) (see recipe in Sauces and Toppings) or 1 squirt of
almond milk (non-dairy) whipped cream

Preparation:

1. Mix flax meal, pumpkin pie spice, and arrowroot in small bowl.

2. In a blender, combine the eggs, pumpkin, almond butter,
coconut oil, and dry ingredients. Blend on high until just combined.

3. Warm a little coconut oil in large skillet or griddle on medium-low heat.

4. Add batter in small circles and watch closely; batter will cook very
quickly. Flip pancakes after 30 to 45 seconds. Be sure to keep
pancakes small to cook more evenly and prevent them from burning.

5. Add the whipped cream and coconut sugar or maple syrup, if desired. Yum!

Super Simple Tanana Pancakes

My grandson, Liam, calls me Tanana. That's all it takes to make me melt. I named these pancakes in dedication to him. He loves them, and I bet your kids will love them too.

Makes about 8-10 small pancakes

Ingredients:

1 cup fresh strawberries, stems removed

3 eggs

1 banana

1 teaspoon almond butter

1 teaspoon coconut oil

2 tablespoons flax meal

1 teaspoon arrowroot

1 teaspoon coconut sugar or maple syrup (optional)

1 tablespoon Rapturous Coconut Whipped Cream (optional) (see recipe in Sauces and Toppings) or 1 squirt of almond milk (non-dairy) whipped cream

Preparation:

1. In advance, blend strawberries in a high-speed blender until mixture is a sauce-like consistency. Place sauce in a small serving bowl and set aside. Rinse blender.

2. Place all ingredients for pancakes in blender and blend on medium speed for 30 seconds or until mixture is smooth. (Instead of using a blender, you may place ingredients in a bowl and use a handheld mixer.)

3. Heat a large ceramic nonstick pan or griddle sprayed with a light coat of coconut oil over medium-low heat.

4. Ladle small circles of batter onto the heated pan, about 3 inches in diameter (about the size of an average can top). If you make them too large, they will burn and be difficult to turn. Watch closely, as they cook quickly, usually about 30 to 45 seconds per side.

5. Plate pancakes and spoon a small amount of strawberry sauce over the top and add the whipped cream, if desired.

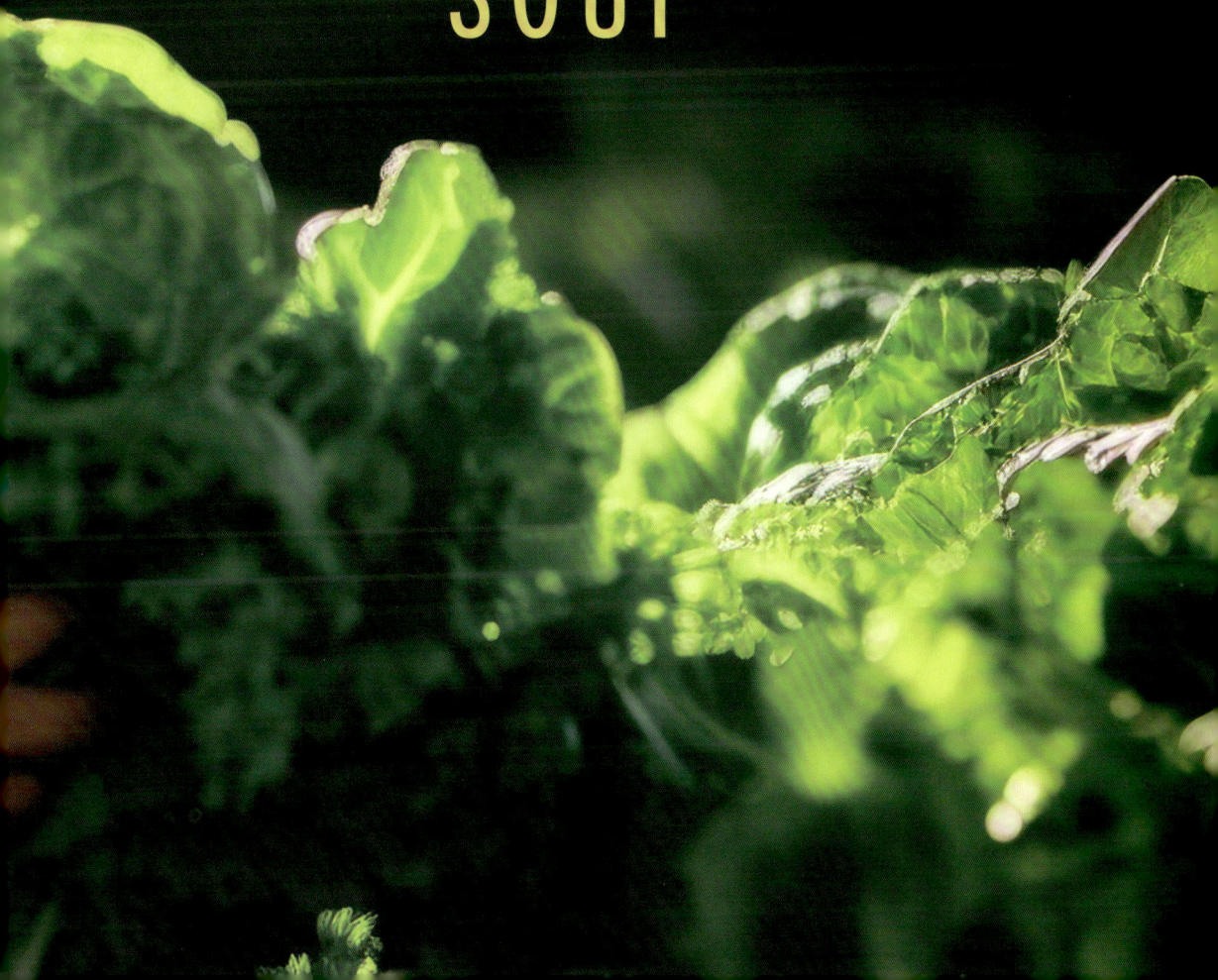

LIGHT

SALADS

&

SOUP

Happy Apple Crunch Salad

Serves 4

Salad Ingredients:

4-6 cups mixed greens
   (spinach, romaine, chard, kale, etc.)

½ cup apple, cored and julienned
   or diced small

1 cup carrot, peeled and julienned
   or diced small

1 cup cucumber, peeled, julienned
   or diced small

½ cup walnuts

Optional herbs to enhance the flavor
   of the greens: basil, mint, or parsley

Vinaigrette Ingredients:

2 teaspoons rice wine vinegar
   (sodium-and sugar-free or any
   vinegar you prefer)

2 teaspoons olive oil

¼ teaspoon minced garlic

½ teaspoon raw organic honey

Preparation:

1. Whisk together the rice wine vinegar, olive oil, garlic, and honey and set aside.

2. Mix apple, carrot, cucumber, walnuts, greens, and herbs (optional) for the salad.

3. Toss salad mixture with the vinaigrette and divide among four plates.

Gratitude Grapefruit Caesar Salad

Serves 4

Salad Ingredients:

6 cups mixed greens

1 pink grapefruit, peeled, seeded and diced large

⅓ cup pumpkin seeds or almonds

¼ cup pomegranate seeds (optional)

1 teaspoon garlic powder

Dressing Ingredients:

Juice of ½-1 pink grapefruit (about ¼-½ cup)

¼ avocado, peeled and pitted

¼-½ teaspoon minced garlic

⅛ teaspoon salt and ground black pepper combined (optional)

Cold water

Preparation:

1. In a blender, puree pink grapefruit juice, avocado, garlic, salt, and pepper to a creamy dressing consistency. If it is too thick, add a little cold water 1 teaspoon at a time or a little more juice.

2. You may use pumpkin seeds or almonds raw with garlic powder, or toast the pumpkin seeds or almonds and garlic powder until just golden in a sauté pan over medium heat. Set aside to cool.

3. Toss the greens, grapefruit, and pomegranate (optional) with the dressing and top with pumpkin seeds or almonds. Enjoy!

Warm Quinoa Spinach Salad

This is a great meal option for breakfast or lunch. I usually double the portion so I have leftovers for the next morning. It is a great "breakfast on the run" if you're really busy.

Serves 6

Ingredients:

3-4 tablespoons vegetable broth
   for sautéing, or 2 teaspoons refined
   coconut oil

¼ cup onion, peeled and finely diced

4 garlic cloves, minced or 2 teaspoons
   pre-minced, jarred garlic

1 tablespoon refined coconut oil

1 cup quinoa, rinsed

2 cups vegetable broth or water

1 bunch asparagus tips

2 handfuls fresh spinach, chopped

1 tablespoon fresh sage,
   or 1 teaspoon dried

2 tablespoons fresh chopped chives,
   or 1 teaspoon dried ¼ cup
   raw pine nuts

2 tablespoons Bragg Liquid
   Aminos (optional)

Preparation:

1. Heat vegetable broth or 2 teaspoons coconut oil in large pot over medium heat. Add onions and sauté for 1 minute.

2. Add garlic and sauté for an additional minute.

3. Add 1 tablespoon of coconut oil to garlic and onions. Add quinoa and stir well to coat lightly with oil.

4. Turn heat up to medium high and stir quinoa constantly for about 10 minutes or until quinoa is lightly toasted.

5. Add 2 cups vegetable broth or water and increase heat to high. Bring to a boil. Reduce heat to medium low and simmer for 15 minutes or until liquid is absorbed.

6. Add asparagus tips to quinoa during last 2 minutes of cooking. This will give you crunchy asparagus and ensure that they are not overcooked. If you prefer softer veggies, you may steam or sauté them separately and add them.

7. Mix the spinach into the quinoa while the quinoa is still warm. It will wilt the spinach without overcooking it, thus retaining most of the nutritional value.

8. Optional: You may want to toss salad with 1 tablespoon of refined coconut oil or olive oil to give the salad a nice texture.

9. Add sage, chives, and pine nuts and stir well. Add salt and pepper to taste.

10. Season with Bragg Liquid Aminos, if desired, and serve warm.

Creamy Butternut Squash Soup

The most time-consuming part of this recipe is chopping the butternut squash. Fortunately, many stores now offer pre-chopped, organic squash. It's a great time-saver in a pinch. Using the crock pot is one of my favorite hacks. Just throw everything in, wait a couple hours and… voila! It's also a great way to get kids involved because it's so simple. Since most kids like the sweet taste of butternut squash and sweet potato, using them as a base can be a great way to create a healthy meal. In general, soups have always been one of my favorite ways to sneak in some extra nutrition with pureed vegetables, herbs, and spices.

Serves 4

Ingredients:

4-5 cups chopped butternut squash

2 cups organic vegetable broth or bone broth

3-4 garlic cloves, peeled

1 green apple (you can peel or just leave the peel and blend)

½ teaspoon salt or to taste

1 cup full fat coconut milk

1 sweet onion, diced (gives the soup a heartier flavor) (optional)

½ teaspoon cinnamon (optional)

¼ teaspoon nutmeg (optional)

Pinch of white pepper (optional)

2 tablespoons almond slivers (optional)

Preparation:

1. Add all ingredients except coconut milk to a crockpot. Cook for 6-8 hours on low or 2-3 hours on high.

2. When squash is soft and easy to smash with a fork, transfer to a blender bowl, or leave in crock pot and use a hand-held immersion blender. Puree until smooth.

3. Add coconut milk and blend in.

4. Add to bowls.

5. For older kids without nut allergies, top with a few slivered almonds and dust lightly with cinnamon.

Ease Your Mind Asparagus Soup

Serves 6

Ingredients:

1 pound asparagus

1-2 tablespoons ghee or refined coconut oil

½ onion, peeled and diced

1 leek chopped, white and light green parts only (optional)

¼ cup celery, chopped

1 teaspoon dried tarragon, or 1 tablespoon fresh, chopped

3 cups low-sodium vegetable or chicken stock

1 tablespoon arrowroot or rice flour (or any gluten-free flour) dissolved in water

2 tablespoons full-fat coconut milk (optional)

Sea salt and pepper to taste

Preparation:

1. Cut off asparagus tips and reserve. Discard tough ends (the last two inches); chop remaining stems into 2-inch segments.

2. In medium soup pot heat ghee or oil. Sauté onions, leeks, celery, and asparagus stems (not tips) over medium heat for about 5 minutes.

3. Add arrowroot and stir until well blended. Stir continuously for about 1 minute more.

4. Transfer vegetables and flour mixture to a blender. Add about 1 cup stock (enough to help mixture blend easily). Blend well and transfer back to pot.

5. Add remaining stock to pot gradually, stirring out any lumps. Bring soup mixture to a boil then reduce heat and simmer until the soup is smooth and thickened, about 30 to 40 minutes. Stir frequently.

6. Add coconut milk, if desired, for a creamy consistency. Add salt and pepper to taste.

7. Add asparagus tips to soup and simmer 5 to 10 minutes.

8. Add tarragon for flavor.

9. Serve warm.

Cozy Cream of Broccoli Soup

Serves 8

Ingredients:

3 cups plus 2 tablespoons (for sautéing) low-sodium vegetable broth

1 small onion, peeled and roughly chopped

1 celery stalk, roughly chopped

8 cups broccoli florets

½ teaspoon allspice

¼ teaspoon black pepper

2 tablespoons ghee or raw
   organic butter

3 tablespoons almond meal
   or gluten-free flour

2 cups unsweetened almond milk

Preparation:

1. Heat 2 tablespoons vegetable broth in medium pot over medium-high heat. Sauté onion and celery until tender and translucent, 3 to 4 minutes.

2. Add broccoli and broth; bring to a boil. Reduce heat and simmer for 5 minutes.

3. Carefully pour soup into a blender in batches (do not fill blender bowl more than half full). Start blender on low setting and increase speed to high until soup is creamy and smooth. Return soup to pot as each batch is finished. You may also use a handheld blender and blend soup directly in the pot.

4. Keep soup warm on medium-low heat. Add allspice and pepper.

5. In small saucepan over medium heat, melt ghee or raw organic butter. Slowly add almond meal or gluten-free flour, stirring so it doesn't clump.

6. Add almond milk slowly. Stir until mixture is thick.

7. Add mixture to soup pot and blend well. Serve hot.

ENTRÉE SALADS & SOUP

Brain-Boosting BBQ Chicken Salad

This recipe requires marinating the chicken for best results.

Serves 4

Ingredients:

2 free-range, hormone-free, boneless, skinless chicken breasts (4 ounces each)

1 lime, juiced

¼ cup fresh orange juice

3 garlic cloves, minced

½ teaspoon onion powder

1 teaspoon dried sage or 1 tablespoon fresh sage, chopped

1 teaspoon dry thyme or 1 tablespoon fresh thyme, chopped

½ teaspoon salt

¼ teaspoon pepper

1 red bell pepper, chopped

½ cup celery, chopped

½ cup black beans, drained and rinsed

1 avocado, cut into chunks

3 green onions, chopped

4 cups mixed greens

1 tablespoon olive oil

2 tablespoons fresh lime juice

1 tablespoon cilantro, chopped

Salt and pepper to taste

½ cup sugar-free Nature's Hallow BBQ Sauce (optional)

Preparation:

1. In small bowl, combine lime juice, orange juice, garlic, onion powder, sage, thyme, salt, and pepper.

2. Transfer to a sealable plastic bag. Add chicken, turn to coat, and refrigerate for 2 to 24 hours.

3. When ready to cook, preheat grill to medium-high heat.

4. Grill chicken for about 5 to 7 minutes on each side or until chicken is no longer pink in center. Allow to cool slightly before slicing or chopping.

5. In large bowl, mix olive oil, 2 tablespoons lime juice, and cilantro.

6. Add red bell pepper, celery, black beans, avocado, and green onions. Season with salt and pepper. Gently toss, being careful not to mash the avocado.

7. To serve, place greens on platter and spread chopped veggie and bean mixture over greens. Add slices of grilled chicken across the top.

8. Drizzle sugar-free barbecue sauce over the top, if desired. Best served with salad cold and chicken warm.

Pomegranate Pepita Salad with Salmon

Serves 4

Salmon Ingredients:

4 filets wild salmon, skin off;
   4 to 6 ounces each

1 garlic clove, minced

1 teaspoon minced cilantro

½ teaspoon cumin

½ teaspoon paprika

⅛ teaspoon salt

⅛ teaspoon ground black pepper

1 teaspoon extra-virgin coconut oil

2-3 tablespoons low-sodium
   vegetable broth

Salad Ingredients:

12 ounces organic mixed salad greens

½ cup pomegranate seeds

½ cup pepitas or pumpkin seeds,
   raw and unsalted

1 cup carrots, shredded or diced small

1 cup cucumbers diced small

Dressing Ingredients:

¼ cup organic, no-sugar-added
   pomegranate juice

3 tablespoons extra-virgin olive oil

Preparation:

1. Preheat grill to medium.
   (Consider using a stove-top
   grill for smaller portions.)

2. In medium to large dish, combine
   garlic, cilantro, cumin, paprika, salt,
   pepper, coconut oil, and vegetable
   broth; add salmon and marinate.
   Set salmon aside to marinate
   until ready to cook.

3. Toss mixed greens, pomegranate
   seeds, pepitas or pumpkin seeds,
   carrots, and cucumbers and place
   on large serving platter or divide
   evenly between four salad bowls.

4. Serve the dressing lightly whisked
   on the side or toss with the salad.

5. Grill salmon approximately 4 to 5
   minutes per side, depending on the
   thickness of the filets, until they
   begin to flake easily.

6. Serve salmon over the salad
   and enjoy!

Watermelon Mint Salad with Grilled Shrimp

This is a classic favorite in the Amen house with all the kids. The best thing about salads is adding all your favorite things and swapping things you don't like. Since we have a big family, with many varying preferences, I often set up a large lazy Susan style buffet and allow everyone to add what they prefer. For this recipe, consider adding bolder flavors as your child's palate evolves. We love adding a curry flavor to shrimp. Or you can add 1 teaspoon of oregano and a pinch of paprika. I encourage you to play with flavor.

Serves 4

Shrimp Ingredients:

Wooden skewers

1 pound large shrimp, peeled and deveined

3 tablespoons avocado oil or macadamia nut oil

2 tablespoons lemon juice

½ teaspoon salt

¼ teaspoon black pepper (optional)

½ teaspoon garlic powder

Salad Ingredients:

4-6 cups chopped romaine or
lettuce of your choice

¼ cup mint leaves

¼ cup mint leaves

¼ cup roughly chopped basil
(optional)

1 small cucumber, sliced

2-3 cups watermelon, cubed
(4-5 small cubes per plate)

½ cup crumbled goat cheese
(optional)

1 cup grape tomatoes or some
chopped bell pepper
(optional)

Salad Dressing Ingredients:

¼ cup balsamic vinegar

2-3 tablespoons extra virgin
olive oil

Pinch of sea salt

Preparation:

1. Soak skewers while preparing
shrimp.

2. In a large bowl whisk
together oil, lemon juice, salt,
pepper, and garlic powder.

3. Add the shrimp and gently
toss, coating with marinade.
Marinate in refrigerator for
at least 15-30 minutes.

4. While shrimp is marinating make
salad dressing by whisking together
all ingredients and prepare salad.
Place a layer of lettuce on each
plate and add in mint, cucumbers,
and basil (if desired). Add other
vegetables of your choice. Top with
watermelon and sprinkle goat
cheese (if desired). Drizzle a small
amount of dressing over the top.

5. Using wooden skewers, thread 4-6
shrimp on each soaked skewer and
place on a plate while skewering the
remaining shrimp.

6. Heat a grill or grill pan over
medium-high heat and cook the
shrimp for about 2 minutes on
each side until the color is pink
and shrimp is opaque. Cook time
depends on size of shrimp and
how hot the grill is.

7. Remove shrimp from skewers and
place on top of salads.

Sesame Citrus Kale Salad with Chicken

Serves 6

Ingredients:

8 ounces organic kale, shredded

¼-½ cup cilantro, chopped

2 cara cara or navel oranges, 1 juiced for dressing
   and 1 peeled and diced for salad

¼ teaspoon sea salt

½ teaspoon ground pepper

1 teaspoon organic honey

1 tablespoon toasted sesame oil

⅛ cup golden raisins

2 tablespoons toasted sesame seeds

2 tablespoons raw pecans, roughly chopped

3 cups grilled or baked free-range, hormone-free,
   antibiotic-free chicken, chopped

Preparation:

1. Place kale and cilantro in large bowl.

2. In small bowl, whisk together the juice of 1 orange, sea salt, ground pepper,
   honey, and sesame oil. Whisk until blended.

3. Toss diced orange, raisins, sesame seeds, pecans, and dressing with
   the kale and cilantro. Refrigerate for 30 minutes prior to serving.

4. Serve salad on plates and top with chicken. Enjoy!

Snappy Shrimp and Mango Salad

Serves 4

Shrimp Ingredients:

1 pound shrimp, peeled and de-veined

1 tablespoon minced garlic

1 teaspoon finely chopped parsley

⅛ teaspoon sea salt

⅛ teaspoon ground black pepper

1 teaspoon extra-virgin coconut oil

Salad Ingredients:

12 ounces organic mixed greens

1 cup cilantro, roughly chopped

1 cup cucumber, diced

½ cup mango, diced

1 cup red bell pepper, diced

½ cup red onion, peeled and diced

1 avocado, diced or quartered

Dressing Ingredients:

½ cup light coconut milk

2 tablespoons lime juice

1 tablespoon raw organic honey

½ teaspoon minced garlic

⅛ teaspoon sea salt

⅛ teaspoon ground black pepper

1 tablespoon toasted sesame oil

Preparation:

1. Preheat grill to medium. (For smaller dishes, consider a stove top grill pan.)

2. In medium to large bowl, toss shrimp with garlic, parsley, salt, pepper, and coconut oil. You can either grill the shrimp immediately and then refrigerate for a cold salad later or set shrimp aside until ready to grill and serve warm.

3. For dressing, in small bowl, whisk together coconut milk, lime juice, honey, garlic, salt, and pepper. Slowly drizzle in the toasted sesame oil while whisking to combine. The dressing may separate and need to be mixed again before serving. Serve on the side, 1-2 tablespoons per serving.

4. In large bowl, toss the salad greens, cilantro, cucumber, mango, red bell pepper, and red onion. Divide the salad onto four plates and garnish each with ¼ of the avocado.

5. Grill shrimp about 1 minute on each side until they turn pink and start to curl. Remove from grill and divide among salads.

Calming Chicken Lentil Soup

Serves 6

Ingredients:

6¼ cups no-salt-added chicken or vegetable broth, divided

4 celery stalks, cut into ½-inch pieces

1 carrot, peeled and cut into ½-inch pieces

1 red bell pepper, chopped

1 onion, peeled and chopped

2 garlic cloves, minced

6 cups purified water

2 cups red lentils

½ teaspoon curry powder

½ teaspoon ground cumin

1 tablespoon lemon pepper

1 teaspoon pepper

2 cups cooked hormone-free, antibiotic-free, free-range chicken breast, chopped (I use whatever leftovers I have for this soup)

1 tablespoon fresh lemon juice

Optional ingredients:

1 tablespoon fresh marjoram, finely chopped, or 1 teaspoon dried

1 tablespoon fresh sage, finely chopped, or 1 teaspoon dried

1 teaspoon garlic salt (or to taste)

Preparation:

1. In large soup pot, heat ¼ cup chicken or vegetable broth (preferably). Sauté celery, carrot, pepper, onion, and garlic for about 5 minutes.

2. Add water and 6 cups vegetable broth to pot. Stir in lentils. Cover and bring to a boil. Reduce heat and simmer, stirring occasionally, for about 25 minutes.

3. Stir in curry, cumin, lemon pepper, and pepper, and herbs and garlic salt, if desired. Simmer uncovered for about 20 minutes or until lentils fall apart and mixture thickens. Add chicken during the last 5 minutes.

4. Stir in lemon juice.

5. Ladle soup into bowls and serve hot.

Healing Chicken Vegetable Soup

Soups are a favorite in the Amen household. This one is a perfectly satisfying meal for a snowy day—or any day for that matter!

Serves 6

Ingredients:

2 tablespoons coconut oil

2 garlic cloves, minced

1 bay leaf

2 celery stalks, sliced

2 leeks, halved lengthwise and sliced (white part only)

1 carrot, peeled and diced

1 sweet potato, peeled and diced

2 boneless, skinless hormone-free, antibiotic-free chicken breasts (4-6 ounces each), cut into large cubes

1 cup water

5 cups vegetable broth

1 teaspoon onion powder

½ teaspoon dried marjoram

½ teaspoon dried sage

1½ cups green cabbage, shredded

2 tablespoons fresh chopped parsley or 2 teaspoons dried

Salt and pepper to taste

Preparation:

1. In large pot, heat oil over medium high heat. Add garlic, bay leaf, celery, leeks, carrot, and sweet potato and sauté for 2 to 3 minutes, stirring frequently.

2. Add chicken and cook for 4 more minutes.

3. Stir in water, vegetable broth, onion powder, marjoram, and sage. Bring to a boil, reduce heat and simmer for 15 to 20 minutes.

4. Add cabbage and simmer for 5 minutes. Season with salt and pepper as desired.

5. Ladle into soup bowls. Top with parsley and serve hot.

Settling Lentil Lamb Stew

Serves 6

Ingredients:

2 tablespoons grapeseed oil

12 ounces ground hormone-free, antibiotic-free, free-range lamb

½ onion peeled and chopped

2 garlic cloves minced

1 carrot, peeled and diced

1 celery stalk

½ red bell pepper, diced

3 large tomatoes seeded and diced, or one 14-ounce jar low-sodium diced tomatoes

4 cups no-salt-added vegetable broth

1 cup red lentils

½ teaspoon dried rosemary or 1 teaspoon fresh, chopped

½ teaspoon dried fresh thyme or 1 teaspoon fresh, chopped

½ teaspoon dried tarragon or 1 teaspoon fresh, chopped

½ teaspoon sea salt (optional)

Preparation:

1. Heat oil in large stockpot over medium heat. Add lamb, onion, garlic, carrot, celery, and red bell pepper. Cook until lamb is lightly browned, about 3 to 4 minutes, stirring regularly.

2. Add tomatoes, vegetable broth, lentils, herbs, and sea salt. Bring mixture to a boil. Reduce heat and simmer for 30 minutes or until lentils are soft but not mushy

3. Ladle into bowls and serve hot.

Soothing Shrimp Chowder

Serves 6

Ingredients:

2 teaspoons macadamia nut oil or coconut oil

4 small sweet potatoes, diced

1 medium yellow onion, peeled and diced

8 celery stalks, chopped

3 carrots, peeled and chopped

1 14-ounce can coconut milk

2 cups unsweetened almond milk

½ teaspoon Thai green curry paste

½ teaspoon vanilla extract

1 pound fresh shrimp, peeled and deveined (you may choose to remove tails)

1 cup fresh or canned peas

1 cup fresh spinach

½ teaspoon pepper

1 teaspoon sea salt (optional)

Preparation:

1. Heat oil in large skillet over medium high heat. Sauté potatoes, onion, celery, and carrots briefly, about 5 minutes (do not overcook). Add coconut milk, almond milk, green curry paste, and vanilla. Mix well. Turn heat down to simmer for 10 minutes.

2. Add shrimp, peas, spinach, pepper, and salt (optional) to skillet and cook for about 3 to 4 minutes or until shrimp are pink and no longer translucent. Do not overcook or shrimp will become tough.

3. Transfer one-third of entire soup mixture to blender to puree. Transfer pureed mixture back to soup pot and mix well. You may skip this step to save time or if you prefer a thinner soup base. However, this step makes the soup more like chowder. Simmer for 5 minutes.

4. Ladle chowder into bowls and serve hot.

POULTRY

Chloe's Favorite Chicken Wings

Serves 2

Ingredients:

1 dozen free-range chicken wings (I also use mini drumsticks)

2 tablespoons ghee or coconut oil

Spice Blend Ingredients:

1 teaspoon onion powder

½ teaspoon garlic powder

½ teaspoon cinnamon

1 teaspoon ancho or chipotle chili powder

1 teaspoon smoked paprika

½-1 teaspoon sea salt (optional)

½ teaspoon black pepper (optional)

Sauce Options:

Serve chicken wings with Zesty Aioli Sauce (see recipe in Sauces and Toppings) or Distinctive Onion Dill Ranch Dressing (see recipe in Sauces and Toppings).

Preparation:

1. Preheat oven to 375˚F.

2. Blend spices together in small mixing bowl.

3. Place chicken wings in large mixing bowl and toss with spice blend. Be sure to cover all pieces with a light coat of the spice blend.

4. Place chicken in baking dish and bake for approximately 30 minutes.

5. Serve hot.

Comforting Cashew Cream Turkey and Squash

Serves 4

Ingredients:

1 pound free-range, hormone-free, antibiotic-free ground turkey

1 poblano chili

1 pound yellow and green summer squash, diced

1 teaspoon sea salt (optional)

1 tablespoon macadamia nut oil or grapeseed oil

2-4 tablespoons low-sodium vegetable broth for sautéing (or 2 teaspoons of grapeseed oil)

1 cup red or orange bell peppers, diced

½ cup sweet onion, peeled and diced

½ cup cashew cream sauce (see recipe below)

Preparation for Cashew Cream Sauce:

1. To make cashew cream, rinse 2 cups of raw cashews under cold water. Put the cashews in a bowl and cover with cold water. Cover bowl and refrigerate overnight.

2. The next day, drain the cashews and rinse under cold water.

3. Place cashews in a blender with enough fresh cold water to cover by 1 inch. Using a high-powered blender, blend on high for several minutes until mixture becomes a smooth cream.

Preparation:

1. Preheat oven to 400° F.

2. Lightly rub poblano chili with oil. Roast for about 15 minutes on baking sheet. Skin should blister. Remove from oven and cool. Rub skin off. Cut pepper open, remove seeds, and dice pepper.

3. In a colander, toss the squash with 1 teaspoon sea salt if desired. Let stand over a plate or in the sink for 30 minutes, then rinse. Let dry on paper towels.

4. While squash is resting, heat oil in large pan over medium heat. Lightly brown ground turkey, stirring frequently, about 7 to 8 minutes. Turn off heat and set aside. Do not overcook.

5. Heat a tablespoon of broth over medium-high heat. Sauté squash until browned and tender. Add a tablespoon of broth as needed to prevent burning, about 5 to 7 minutes. Remove squash; discard broth.

6. In same pan used for squash, reduce heat to medium. Add another tablespoon of broth as necessary. Add the bell peppers, chili, and onion. Stir regularly until the onion is soft or lightly browned, about 3 to 5 minutes. Drain off extra broth.

7. Add cashew cream. Simmer until cream is reduced to a thick sauce, about 10 to 15 minutes.

8. Add squash and turkey to the cream mixture and blend well.

Grilled Rosemary Chicken

Serves 4

Ingredients:

4 organic, skinless chicken breasts (4-6 ounces each)

1-2 tablespoons minced garlic

1 tablespoon minced parsley

1 tablespoon minced rosemary

2 teaspoons grapeseed oil

⅛ teaspoon salt and ground black pepper combined (optional)

Preparation:

1. Heat grill. (Consider using a stove-top grill for smaller portions.)

2. In medium to large bowl, rub chicken breasts with garlic, parsley, rosemary, and grapeseed oil. Add salt and pepper, if desired. Hold until ready to cook.

3. Grill chicken about 4 to 5 minutes on each side until fully cooked. Chop or slice chicken.

4. If desired, add the chicken to the Gratitude Grapefruit Caesar Salad.

Guiltless Chicken Tenders

Serves 4

Ingredients:

1 teaspoon sea salt

½ teaspoon pepper (optional)

½ teaspoon garlic powder

1 cup almond meal or gluten-free flour,
or you may grind almonds finely in
the food processor

1 pound free-range, hormone-free,
antibiotic-free chicken tenders

1 egg, cage-free, lightly beaten

2-3 tablespoons ghee or refined
coconut oil for frying (optional)
Honey mustard sauce (optional)

Preparation:

1. Preheat oven to 375˚F.

2. In shallow bowl, mix sea salt, pepper
(optional), garlic powder, and almond
meal (or gluten-free flour) and blend
well with a fork.

3. Dip chicken pieces in the egg,
coating both sides. Immediately
dredge in the almond meal mixture,
covering both sides completely.

4. Place chicken on a baking sheet.
Cook for about 12 minutes, turning
chicken over after 6 minutes.

Note: These chicken tenders will not be crispy.
If you are used to fried chicken tenders,
you may want to finish with one more step:

5. Heat 2-3 tablespoons coconut oil in
large skillet over medium-high heat.
When skillet is hot, add half of the
baked tenders to skillet. Cook for
about 30 to 60 seconds per side
until lightly browned. Remove
tenders and repeat process for
remaining chicken tenders. Allow
to cool for several minutes if
serving to children.

Honey Mustard Sauce Preparation:

1. Mix 1 tablespoon gluten-free
mustard with 1 teaspoon of raw,
unfiltered honey. Note: Raw,
unfiltered honey is not appropriate
for children under 2 years of age

Use pasteurized honey in recipes
for children under age 2.

Turkey Tacos

Serves 4

You can make these tacos with grain-free taco shells or as a low-carb option by turning it into a bowl. For this recipe, prepare all toppings first, then make the meat and cauliflower rice simultaneously to save time.

Taco Meat Ingredients:

1-2 tablespoon avocado oil

1 pound ground turkey meat, free-range, organic

½ cup sweet onion, chopped

2-3 garlic cloves, minced

1 pack of Siete brand taco seasoning mix (or another clean brand)

Rice Ingredients:

1 bag cauliflower rice (Trader Joe's is my favorite)

Note: The following are optional to your (and your child's) taste.

Pinch of taco seasoning, simple spices, or salt and pepper

1-2 tsp avocado oil

1 tsp onion powder (to taste)

1 tsp garlic powder

Salt and pepper to taste

Salsa Ingredients:

Note: I often opt for pre-made queso salsa from Primal Kitchen. It's clean and low carb. However, it's pretty simple to make fresh salsa if you choose. If you prefer a low-carb version, you can swap the tomatoes for red bell peppers. Or you can try a mango salsa for your munchkin if they won't eat tomatoes. Just watch the sugar content.

1 15-ounce can tomatoes

½ can Ortega Chiles
   (or another variety that isn't too hot)

½ cup cilantro

1 lime

¼ teaspoon salt or to taste

Toppings Ingredients:

Note: These are all optional to your (and your child's) taste.

1 avocado, sliced or chopped

½ cup green onion, chopped

½ cup chopped cilantro

½ cup crumbled goat cheese or
   vegan cheese for a dairy-free option

Other Optional Ingredients:

16 large romaine lettuce leaves,
   washed and dried

4-8 Siete brand taco shells

Toppings Preparation:

1. Slice avocado, chop onion, and prepare cheese as preferred. Set aside.

2. Prepare salsa or pour pre-made salsa into a bowl.

3. Prepare taco bowls, shells, or romaine leaves as desired and plate. Set aside.

Taco Meat Preparation:

1. In a large skillet heat the oil over medium heat.

2. Add onions and garlic. Sautee for 2 minutes.

3. Add turkey. Break apart with wooden spoon or spatula. Turn and mix until meat is browned, usually about 3-4 min.

4. Add taco seasoning and blend into meat, turning and mixing frequently.

5. Reduce heat to low until rice is finished.

Rice Preparation:

Note: I like to cook cauliflower rice at higher temp than usually suggested, and I keep it dry. I only add a little oil if it looks like it might burn. I do this so it cooks faster and stays crisper. If you're using frozen rice, it will already have a lot of moisture. The longer you cook cauliflower rice, and the more moisture you add, the mushier it becomes. I prefer to almost brown it, then quickly remove it from the heat.

1. Heat medium pan over medium-high heat.

2. Add cauliflower rice.

3. Sprinkle desired spices over rice.

4. Turn and mix frequently with a wooden spoon or spatula so rice doesn't burn, usually about 4-5 minutes. Test for doneness. Remove from heat and put in bowls ready to serve.

Assembly Preparation:

1. Put rice in bowls, shells, or lettuce leaves.

2. Add a small amount of taco meat (for bowls divide into quarters)

3. Add desired toppings: avocado, onion, cilantro, cheese, etc. I section toppings but you can also mix it up like a salad.

4. Top with salsa.

Spiced Cacao Turkey Chili

Serves 8

Ingredients:

1 tablespoon refined coconut oil

1 pound lean ground free-range, hormone-free, antibiotic-free turkey

1 cup chopped onion

3 garlic cloves, chopped

1 teaspoon chili powder

1 small can Ortega green chilies

1 tablespoon fresh oregano or 1 teaspoon dried

1 tablespoon raw cacao powder

1 teaspoon cinnamon

1 teaspoon cumin seed

1-2 teaspoons sea salt

3 cups diced tomatoes, fresh (preferably) or organic canned (no-salt-added variety)

2 cups chicken or vegetable broth

2 cups chopped celery

1 cup chopped red bell peppers

½ cup chopped zucchini

2 cups dried kidney beans, cooked and drained (you may use canned if you don't have time to cook beans)

1 cup black beans or chickpea beans, cooked

1 jalapeno pepper, chopped (optional, makes chili pretty spicy)

Preparation:

1. In large saucepan or pot over medium heat, add refined coconut oil and brown turkey meat. Crumble turkey and break apart as much as possible. Add onion and stir for about 2 minutes.

2. Add garlic, chili powder, Ortega chilies, oregano, cacao, cinnamon, cumin seed, salt, tomatoes, and jalapeno, if desired. Mix thoroughly until spices are well blended with meat and meat is lightly browned (about 3 minutes).

3. Add broth and bring to a boil, then reduce heat and simmer for 5 minutes.

4. Dish out 2 cups of chili mixture. Put about one cup of chili at a time into the blender. Add 1 cup celery, ½ cup of chopped bell pepper, and ¼ cup zucchini at a time and purée. Pour each mixture back into the remaining chili pot. Adding the pureed vegetables not only makes the chili tasty, but is also a great way to add fiber and vitamins without overcooking.

5. Add the beans. Stir thoroughly and heat through on medium-low, about 5 minutes. Serve hot.

SEAFOOD

Coconut Shrimp

Coconut shrimp is traditionally a kid favorite, but it's often loaded with sugar. I've found that it's still quite tasty even without the sugar. If your kids prefer a sweeter taste, you can always add a touch of monk fruit to the batter. Adding honey improves the flavor but also increases the sugar content.

Serves 4

Ingredients:

12-16 raw jumbo shrimp

2 eggs

1 cup shredded coconut (I like the coarse, long-shredded coconut)

1 ½ cup coconut flour (almond flour also works)

1 teaspoon sea salt

1 teaspoon garlic powder

Pinch of pepper (optional)

1 tablespoon monk fruit (optional)

½-1 cup macadamia nut oil or coconut oil

Preparation:

1. Butterfly shrimp, wash, pat dry and set aside

2. In a medium size bowl, whisk eggs until yolks and whites are blended.

3. In a second bowl dry whisk coconut flour, shredded coconut, salt, garlic powder, and optional ingredients as desired.

4. Dip each shrimp into egg, then coat lightly with flour mixture and place on cookie sheet or plate. Keep a damp cloth nearby to wipe fingers after dipping. Continue until all shrimp are dipped and coated in flour.

5. In a large pan, add ¼-½ cup oil (enough to fry all shrimp, depending on size of pan and number of shrimp). Heat oil over medium-high heat for about 1 or 2 minutes, or until pan is completely hot.

6. Add about half of the shrimp to avoid overcooking. They cook fast! Turn after about a minute. Cook for about 2-3 minutes total, depending on the size of the shrimp. Shrimp should no longer be opaque in the center when cooked. Remove and place on serving platter. If necessary, add more oil. Add remaining shrimp and repeat.

7. For young children, allow to cool for a couple minutes and serve warm.

Cashew Crusted Sea Bass With Butternut Squash Puree

Serves 4

Fish Ingredients:

4 pieces sea bass (4 ounces each) or substitute your favorite wild-caught fish

2 tablespoons raw minced cashews (easiest in a food processor)

1 tablespoons minced garlic

2-3 tablespoons fresh herbs (oregano, marjoram, parsley, or chives) or 1 teaspoon dried

1 tablespoon lemon zest

1 teaspoon salt and ground pepper combined (optional)

Butternut Squash Puree

Ingredients:

1⅓-2 cups butternut squash, peeled, chopped, boiled until tender, drained and set aside)

¼-½ cup almond milk (plain, unsweetened)

⅛ teaspoon monk fruit

¼ teaspoon nutmeg

Sauce Ingredients:

4 cups low-sodium vegetable broth

Preparation:

1. Heat oven to 375° F.

2. In a food processor, chop cashews, garlic, herbs, and lemon zest to create a crumble topping. Add salt and pepper, if desired.

3. Place the sea bass on a sheet pan lined with parchment paper. Top each portion equally with the cashew-herb crumble and refrigerate until ready to cook.

4. In medium saucepan over medium-high heat, bring broth to a boil, then reduce heat to medium. Reduce vegetable broth until it is similar in consistency to light gravy. This may take 20- 30 minutes. Keep warm.

5. In a food processor or with a hand mixer, combine the cooked butternut squash, ¼ cup almond milk, monk fruit, and nutmeg. Blend until smooth. (Add additional almond milk if necessary.) Warm mixture in saucepan over medium-low heat and set aside until ready to serve. Stir occasionally.

6. Bake the fish about 8 to 12 minutes, until it is cooked and flakes easily.

7. Place a scoop of butternut puree on each plate; top with sea bass. Drizzle vegetable broth sauce over fish and serve.

Fat Head Fish Sticks

Serves 4

Ingredients:

1 to 1½ pounds of wild halibut (or other white fish), skinned and deboned

1 cup macadamia nuts

½ cup coconut or almond flour

½ teaspoon onion powder

½ teaspoon garlic powder

2-3 eggs, cage free

3 tablespoons ghee or refined coconut oil for frying

½ teaspoon sea salt (optional)

Preparation:

1. Place macadamia nuts in a food processor bowl. Grind until nuts are finely chopped, but not to the consistency of flour or meal; mixture should remain course. If you over mix, the natural oils will emerge, and the mixture will begin to clump. Once nuts are finely chopped, place them in a bowl.

2. Mix coconut flour, onion powder, and garlic powder in wide, shallow bowl.

3. In separate bowl, whisk eggs thoroughly.

4. Line up bowls: coconut flour mixture first, then egg, then macadamia nuts.

5. Prepare two cookie sheets. Line one cookie sheet with parchment paper. Prepare a second sheet with layers of paper towels to place fish sticks on after cooking. The paper towels will absorb excess oil.

6. Cut halibut into 2-inch strips. Rinse and pat dry with paper towels.

7. Gently place fish sticks in coconut flour, lightly dusting on all sides.

8. Next, dip fish sticks in egg, covering all sides.

9. Finally, roll in ground macadamia nuts and place on cookie sheet with parchment paper.

10. When all the fish sticks are prepared, heat 2 tablespoons of ghee in large skillet over medium heat. When oil is hot, place fish sticks in skillet and cook for approximately 1 minute on each side. Turn, making sure to cook evenly on all sides. Turn again. Fish sticks should cook for approximately 1½ minutes to 2 minutes per side or until golden brown. Add more oil as necessary. The thinner the cut of fish, the faster they will cook.

11. Remove fish sticks and place on cookie sheet with paper towels to absorb excess oil. Salt and pepper as desired.

Grilled Halibut with Roasted Bell Pepper Sauce

Serves 4

Fish Ingredients:

4 skinless halibut fillets
   (4-6 ounces each)

2 garlic cloves, minced

1 tablespoon minced parsley
   or any herbs of choice

⅛ teaspoon salt

⅛ teaspoon ground black pepper

1-2 teaspoons refined coconut oil

2-3 tablespoons low-sodium
   vegetable broth

Sauce Ingredients:

2 large roasted red bell peppers,
   seeds removed

1 large shallot, chopped

½-1 cup low-sodium vegetable broth

Preparation:

1. Preheat grill. (Consider using a stove-top grill for smaller servings.)

2. In small sauté pan, caramelize the shallots over medium heat, adding the vegetable broth a tablespoon at a time until tender.

3. In a food processor, blend the roasted red bell peppers and sautéed shallots until pureed. If the mixture seems too thick, add a couple tablespoons of vegetable broth until it reaches a nice, thick soup consistency. Place the mixture back in the small sauté pan and set aside.

4. In medium to large bowl, combine garlic, parsley, salt, pepper, coconut oil, and vegetable broth. Add halibut fillets, rub with broth mixture, and mainate until ready to cook.

5. Grill fish approximately 4 to 5 minutes per side until it flakes easily.

6. Warm pureed sauce over medium-low heat.

7. Place halibut fillets on a plate and drizzle the bell pepper sauce over the top. Enjoy.

Happy Brain Halibut with Pesto Cream Sauce

Serves 4

Fish Ingredients:

4 halibut fillets (4 ounces each)

1 teaspoon grapeseed oil

Pesto Cream Ingredients:

¼ cup walnuts

1 teaspoon minced garlic

1 cup fresh basil leaves or ⅓ cup dried

½ cup spinach leaves

1 tablespoon olive oil

¼-⅓ cup almond milk or ½ cup coconut milk

Zest of one lemon (reserve juice to serve with cooked fish)

¼ teaspoon salt and ground pepper combined (optional) (about 2 tablespoons per dish). Enjoy!

Preparation:

1. In a food processor or blender, prepare pesto cream by blending walnuts, garlic, basil, and spinach for 30 seconds. Add salt and pepper, if desired.

2. Add olive oil and almond milk (or coconut milk) and blend.

3. Add lemon zest and blend; set aside.

4. Heat grapeseed oil in large sauté pan over medium heat and sear halibut fillets on one side until a golden crust forms and the fish is done on the bottom, 1 to 2 minutes. Gently turn the fish and cover to finish cooking through, about 2 minutes. The fish is ready when it starts to flake.

5. While the fish is cooking, warm pesto cream in a separate small saucepan on medium-low heat and reserve until fish is cooked.

6. Plate the fish, squeeze lemon juice over, if desired, and drizzle the pesto on top (about 2 tablespoons per dish). Enjoy!

Lemon Garlic Shrimp with Cream Sauce

Kids love zoodles! Zucchini noodles are a great pasta alternative that can be purchased at many grocery stores, or they are very simple to make. Young children should not use a zoodle maker without adult supervision as the slicing device is sharp. To make them you will need a zoodle maker, which can be purchased on Amazon or any store that sells culinary supplies. If zoodles aren't an option, you can opt for gluten-free pasta.

Serves 4

Cream Sauce Ingredients:

1-2 tablespoons minced white onions

1-2 teaspoons minced garlic

1 tablespoon arrowroot, rice flour or other gluten-free flour

1 tablespoon refined coconut oil

1⅓ cups full-fat coconut milk (or a little less plain almond milk)

1-2 teaspoons lemon zest

1 tablespoon fresh minced parsley or 1 teaspoon dried

⅛ teaspoon salt and black pepper combined

24 ounces zoodles (see instructions below)

Shrimp Ingredients:

1 pound shrimp, peeled

1-2 teaspoons minced garlic

1 tablespoon fresh minced parsley or 1 teaspoon dried

1 teaspoon lemon zest

⅛ teaspoon salt and black pepper combined

1 tablespoon coconut oil

Preparation:

1. In medium to large bowl, toss shrimp, garlic, parsley, lemon zest, salt, and pepper. Set aside until ready to sauté.

2. In medium saucepan, add coconut oil and over medium heat, sauté white onions. Add garlic and continue to sauté 15 seconds.

3. Add arrowroot or rice flour and whisk 30 seconds to create a light sauce and prevent clumping.

4. While whisking, slowly add coconut milk. Simmer sauce for a couple minutes over low to medium heat, whisking continuously.

5. Add lemon zest, parsley, salt, and pepper. Keep warm on low heat and set aside.

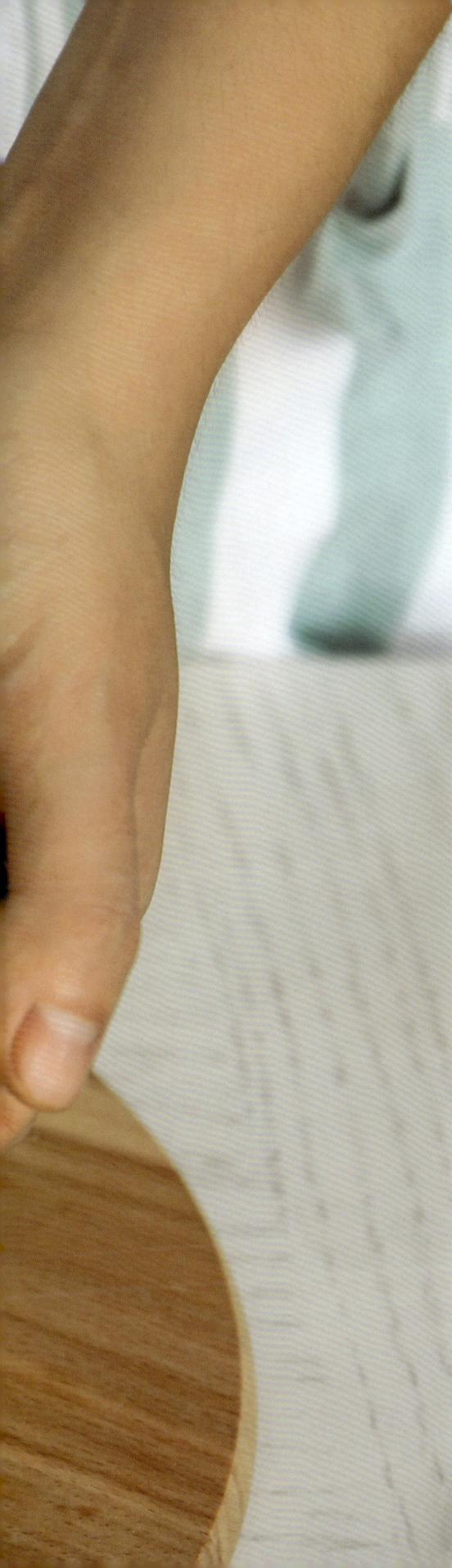

6. In large sauté pan, cook marinated shrimp in coconut oil over medium heat, about 30 seconds on each side (less or more depending on the size of the shrimp) until they are just pink on each side and starting to curl up.

7. Toss the zoodles with the alfredo sauce and divide among four plates. Top with shrimp and a little chopped parsley for garnish. Enjoy.

Zoodles Preparation:

For the simplest way to make thin zucchini noodles you will need a spiralizer, which is now an inexpensive item that can be ordered on Amazon. My favorite is Fullstar. For wider noodles you can also use a potato peeler or a mandolin, but this takes more time.

1. Follow instructions on spiralizer product for desired thickness. Create desired amount of zucchini noodles.

2. Heat about 1-2 teaspoons oil to a medium-size pan. Add noodles and cover for about 30 to 60 seconds (just long enough to heat, but not to cook through or they will be mushy).

Sizzling Shrimp Kabobs

Serves 4

Ingredients:

1 pound shrimp, peeled

2 tablespoons grapeseed oil

1 tablespoon organic honey

2 tablespoons tamari sauce

1 tablespoon gluten-free Dijon mustard

1 teaspoon rice vinegar

3 garlic cloves, minced

½ teaspoon pepper

2 teaspoons fresh chopped thyme or approximately ¾ teaspoon dried

1 red bell pepper, cut into 2-inch pieces

1 small red onion, cut into 2-inch pieces

1 zucchini, cut into 1-inch slices

10 small mushrooms

Wood or stainless steel skewers

Preparation:

1. In large bowl, whisk together oil, honey, tamari sauce, mustard, rice vinegar, garlic, pepper, and thyme.

2. Add shrimp, bell pepper, onion, zucchini, and mushrooms. Toss to coat and refrigerate for up to 24 hours.

3. Lightly oil grill.

4. Thread shrimp and vegetables alternately onto skewers.

5. Place skewers on grill and cook, turning frequently, for about 5 to 8 minutes until shrimp is cooked through (when it turns pink) and vegetables are tender.

MEAT

Meatballs and Zoodles

Serves 4

I love this healthy take on spaghetti and meatballs. It's not only delicious and healthy, but a great way to increase veggies for kids. Fresh sauce doesn't need to be complicated. However, when I'm in a hurry, I use Rao's organic pasta sauce and dress it up with some fresh garlic and basil. It has a lower sugar content than many sauces.

Meatballs Ingredients:

1 pound ground beef or turkey

1 large egg or 2 smaller ones

2 tablespoons Italian seasoning (or add fresh oregano, basil, rosemary, thyme, and marjoram)

½ teaspoon salt or to taste

1 teaspoon garlic powder (optional)

½ cup almond flour or gluten-free breadcrumbs

2 tablespoons low-sodium tamari sauce or coconut aminos

Sauce Ingredients:

2 tablespoons avocado oil or extra virgin olive oil

3-4 garlic cloves, minced

1 28-ounce can whole tomatoes

1 teaspoon dried oregano

½ teaspoon salt or to taste

Pinch of pepper (optional)

Pinch red pepper flakes, if you like spice (optional)

1 teaspoon garlic salt (optional)

½ teaspoon onion powder (optional)

1 tablespoon fresh basil, sliced (optional)

Zoodles Ingredients:

2 large zucchini, if making from scratch (or 1-2 packs of premade Zoodles or 1 box gluten-free pasta)

Sauce Preparation:

Note: I like making the sauce first while I'm preparing the rest of the meal, because the longer it simmers the better it tastes. If using canned sauce, add sauce to medium pot, heat, and add preferred herbs and spices. Let simmer. For fresh sauce prepare as follows:

1. Heat oil in a medium pot over medium heat. Add garlic and sautée for about a minute, being careful not to burn.

2. Add remaining sauce ingredients except fresh basil.

3. Mix and heat through then reduce heat to simmer.

Meatballs Preparation:

1. Preheat oven to 400 degrees F. Line a baking sheet with parchment paper.

2. Using clean hands, combine all ingredients for meatballs into large bowl, making sure to mix evenly through meat. But don't overwork the meat.

3. Using a measuring cup (either ⅓ or ¼ cup size), measure out equal portions of meat, form into round balls, and place on baking sheet. Repeat until all meat is used.

4. Place baking sheet in oven. Check after 15 minutes for meatballs that are less done. Well-done meatballs usually take about 20 minutes.

Zoodles Preparation:

(see instructions in Lemon Garlic Shrimp with Cream Sauce recipe in Seafood)

Note: Prepare zucchini noodles just before serving. If you're using store-bought zucchini noodles, add a small amount of oil to a medium pan and heat for no more than 30 seconds. If you are using gluten-free pasta, prepare according to package and take into account it takes about 10 minutes to prepare.

Assemble Plates:

1. After adding noodles, top each plate with desired number of noodles

2. Spoon a small amount of sauce over each dish.

3. Serve warm.

Easy Does It Bison Steak

This simple recipe is Daniel's favorite, and literally takes minutes to prepare. I've found that my husband isn't alone in his desire for "meat and potatoes." When I do prepare meat, I make sure it is the highest-quality, free-range bison, beef, or lamb I can find. Free-range bison is up to 30 percent lower in palmitic acid (the saturated fat shown to be responsible for heart disease) than industrial-raised beef, and it tastes a whole lot better! But because of the low-fat content, it cooks more rapidly, so you'll want to babysit your steaks while grilling.

Serves 2

Ingredients:

2 free-range bison rib eye or New York cut steaks (8-10 ounces each)

1 tablespoon melted ghee or grapeseed oil

2-3 garlic cloves, mashed

¼-½ teaspoon salt (to taste)

¼-½ teaspoon pepper (to taste)

Preparation:

1. Preheat grill to high.

2. In small bowl, mix melted ghee or oil, garlic, salt, and pepper.

3. Place steaks on plate or tray. Rub oil mixture into steaks on both sides.

4. Place steaks on center of grill for 5 to 7 minutes, then turn and cook for 3 to 4 minutes on the other side. Watch carefully. Every grill cooks differently. I prefer grilling at a higher temperature for less time to sear the steaks and seal the juices. Some people prefer to grill at lower temperatures for longer time. This usually produces a medium to medium-rare steak.

5. Remove steaks from grill, cut in half and place on a serving platter or plates. Reserve leftovers for lunch or use in another recipe the following day. Serve hot.

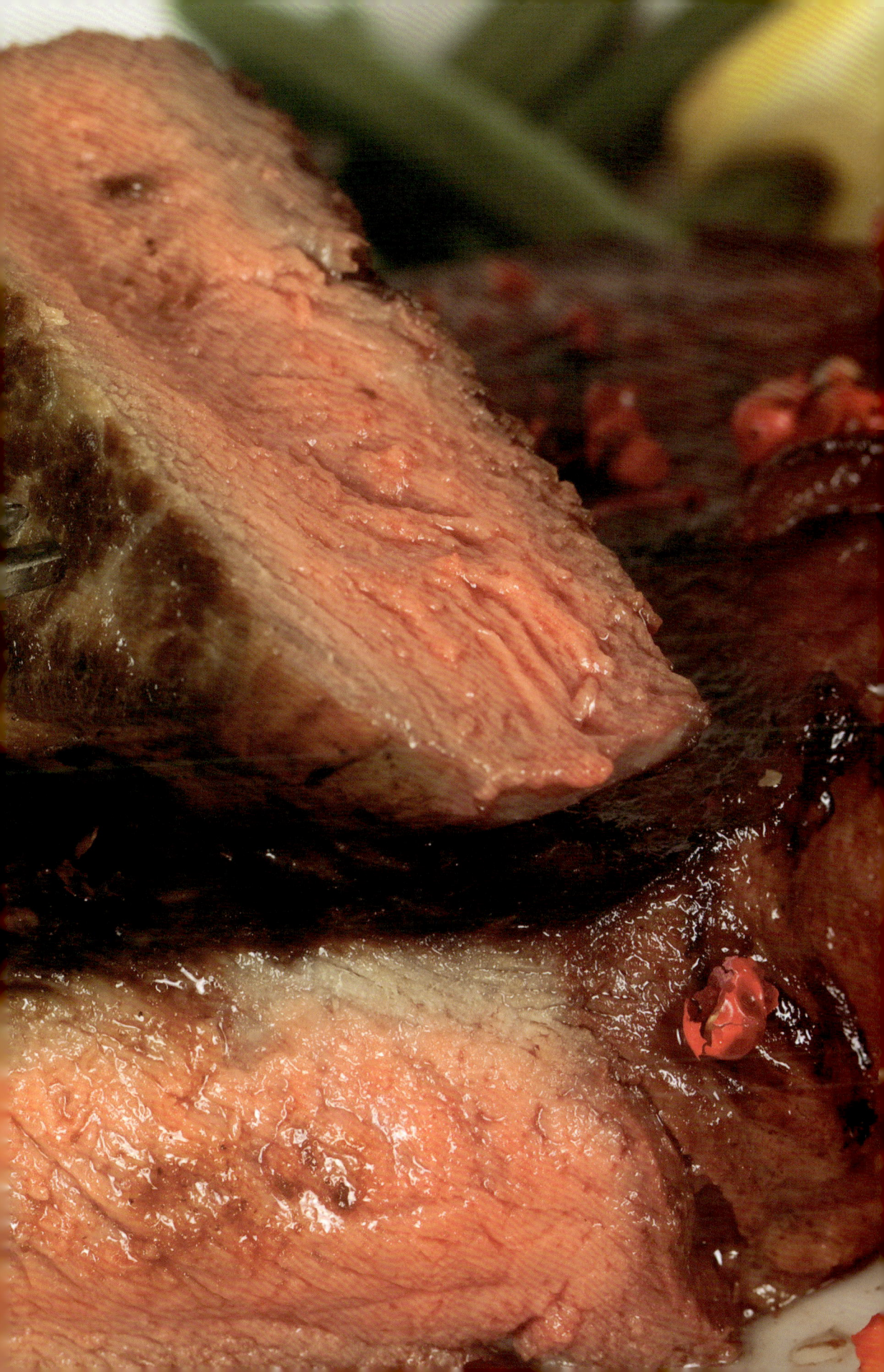

Free-Range Bison Meatloaf

Serves 6

Ingredients:

4 garlic cloves

2 teaspoons dried basil or
2 tablespoons fresh, not chopped

2 teaspoons dried oregano or
2 tablespoons fresh, not chopped

2 teaspoons dried parsley or
2 tablespoons fresh, not chopped

1 teaspoon dried thyme or
1 tablespoon fresh, not chopped
but with thick stems removed
(fine stems are OK)

1 teaspoon dried sage or
1 tablespoon fresh sage,
not chopped

4 celery stalks, cut into 2-inch pieces

1 small onion, peeled and quartered

¼ cup macadamia nuts

¼ cup cashews

2 pounds ground free-range,
hormone free, antibiotic-free
wild bison

1 egg, cage free

2 tablespoons flax meal
(you can grind whole flaxseeds
in a coffee grinder)

¼ teaspoon chili powder

¼ teaspoon black pepper

1 tablespoon low-sodium tamari sauce (you may exclude this for a low-sodium diet)

½ cup no-salt-added organic pasta sauce

Preparation:

1. Preheat oven to 350° F.

2. In a large food processor, place garlic, basil, oregano, parsley, thyme, sage, celery, and onion. Pulse for 15 to 20 seconds, but do not turn on continuous chop setting or mixture will become soggy. Check mixture for consistency. It should be finely chopped with no large pieces, but not mushy. Pulse a few more times if necessary. Remove mixture from food processor and remove any large stray pieces if necessary.

3. Place nuts in food processor. Pulse for 15 to 20 seconds, but do not turn on continuous chop setting or mixture will become pasty. Mixture should be finely chopped with no large pieces, but not sticky or pasty. Pulse a few more times if necessary. Remove mixture from food processor and remove any large stray pieces if necessary.

4. Place bison in large mixing bowl and add egg; mix lightly. Bison is lower in fat than beef and gets tough if you over mix it, so do not overwork the meat.

5. Add herb, onion, and celery mixture to the bowl. Do not mix.

6. Add chopped nuts, flax, chili powder, pepper, and tamari sauce.

7. Mix all ingredients thoroughly through the meat, blending evenly, but being careful not to overwork the meat.

8. Place meat in 9 x 5-inch loaf pan.

9. Place pan on middle oven rack and set timer for 1 hour. It usually takes about 1 ¼ hours to cook.

10. At an hour, check loaf for doneness with a meat thermometer. (Bison is cooked when the internal temperature is 160° F.)

11. Spread pasta sauce over top of meatloaf and return to oven for 15 minutes.

12. Remove from oven and let stand for 5 to 10 minutes before serving.

Mind-Enriching Lamb Meatballs with Zoodles

Something about this combination of spices minimizes the "gaminess" of lamb. Naturally raised lamb is one of the healthiest forms of meat you can eat. Lamb is higher in omega-3 fatty acids than other types of meat.

Serves 4

Ingredients:

1 pound ground grass-fed, hormone free, antibiotic-free, free-range lamb

1 tablespoon grapeseed oil

2 garlic cloves, minced

½ teaspoon cinnamon

1 teaspoon allspice

1 teaspoon cumin (optional)

½ teaspoon garlic salt

¾ cup finely chopped celery

1 28-ounce can stewed tomatoes, low-sodium (or use 4 to 5 cups fresh diced tomatoes to reduce sodium)

½ onion, peeled and chopped

16 ounces zoodles

Preparation:

1. In large bowl, mix lamb, garlic, cinnamon, allspice, cumin (if desired), salt, and celery. Shape into 1-inch meatballs and place onto a tray.

2. Heat oil in skillet over medium heat. Add meatballs to skillet, browning on all sides, about 5 to 10 minutes.

3. Meanwhile, make the tomato sauce. Place tomatoes and onion in a blender bowl. Blend until smooth.

4. Add the sauce to the browned meatballs and simmer for 30 minutes.

5. About 5 minutes before meatballs are finished simmering, boil water in medium saucepan. Prepare the zoodles

6. Divide zoodles evenly onto plates and serve meatballs and sauce over the top.

Savory Lubian Rose Stew

I love the versatility of this recipe. Whether you are a protein lover or a vegetarian, you can adapt this recipe to fit your needs. It is simple, tasty, and nutritious.

Serves 4

Ingredients:

12 ounces lean grass-fed, antibiotic free, hormone-free lamb, chopped into bite-sized pieces

½ cup brown rice (optional)

1 tablespoon refined coconut oil or grapeseed oil

¼ teaspoon salt

¼ teaspoon pepper

½ teaspoon cinnamon

¼ teaspoon allspice

½ small onion, peeled and chopped

8 medium tomatoes, chopped (3 ½ cups) or one 28-ounce can organic diced tomatoes

2 cups fresh green beans

2 tablespoons pine nuts

Preparation:

1. Place rice, if using, in 1 cup boiling water. Add salt, pepper, cinnamon, and allspice to the rice. (If you are not including rice in your meal, add the salt, pepper, cinnamon, and allspice to the lamb in step 3 below.) Cook according to time on package, approximately 20 minutes.

2. In medium-large pan, heat oil over medium heat. Add onions and sauté for 1 minute.

3. Add lamb, salt, pepper, cinnamon, and allspice and cook until meat is lightly browned on all sides, about 5 to 7 minutes. Turn regularly.

4. Add tomatoes. Lower heat, cover, and simmer for 10 minutes.

5. Add green beans and simmer for another 10 minutes (depending on how tender you like the green beans).

6. Serve alone or place rice on serving platter. Serve lamb and tomato mixture over the top. Sprinkle with pine nuts.

Short Ribs for Long Attention

Serves 4

Ingredients:

2 teaspoons dried rosemary
  or 1 tablespoon fresh, chopped

2 teaspoons dried thyme or

1 tablespoon fresh, chopped

1 teaspoon onion powder

1 teaspoon garlic powder

1 teaspoon sea salt

½ teaspoon black pepper

2 pounds free-range bone-in
  beef short ribs

1 tablespoon ghee or coconut oil

1 15-ounce can tomato sauce

⅓ cup red wine vinegar

2 tablespoons organic honey

4-6 garlic cloves (for me more is
  better), mashed with a pestle or
  bottom of a large cup

1 onion, peeled and roughly chopped
  (optional)

2 carrots, peeled and chopped
  (optional)

2 celery stalk, chopped (optional)

Preparation:

1. Prepare slow cooker or crock pot.
   If you don't have a slow cooker, use
   a large cast iron pot and bake in the
   oven on 300°F for 4 to 6 hours.

2. Blend rosemary, thyme, onion
   powder, garlic powder, salt, and
   pepper in small dish.

3. Rub spice mix into ribs, covering
   all sides.

4. In large skillet, heat ghee or oil over
   medium-high heat. Brown ribs for 1
   to 2 minutes on each side.

5. Place ribs in crock pot or slow
   cooker. Add all remaining
   ingredients.

6. Cook on low for 9 hours or on
   medium for 4 to 6 hours. Meat
   should fall off the bone with a fork
   when done.

7. Shred meat from bone or separate
   bones leaving meat on.

8. Ladle vegetables and broth into
   stew bowls. Place ribs or rib meat
   over vegetables. Serve hot.

SIDES

Astute Asparagus

Serves 2

Ingredients:

1 pound asparagus

4 tablespoons low-sodium chicken or vegetable broth

Dressing Ingredients:

2 tablespoons extra-virgin olive oil

1 medium clove garlic, minced

½ teaspoon dried thyme or 1 teaspoon fresh, chopped

½ teaspoon dried rosemary or 1 teaspoon fresh, chopped

2 teaspoons lemon juice

Sea salt and pepper to taste

Dressing Preparation:

1. Mix all ingredients for dressing in small bowl and set aside.

Asparagus Preparation:

1. In a skillet, heat broth over medium heat.

2. While broth is heating, prepare asparagus by cutting or snapping off the hard bottom of asparagus stems (about 2 inches). Cut the trimmed spears into 2-inch pieces.

3. When broth begins to steam, add asparagus. Cover and cook for 3 to 5 minutes.

4. Place asparagus in large bowl and toss with dressing. Serve hot.

Devil-Less Eggs

Serves 6

Ingredients:

12 eggs, cage free
2 tablespoons olive oil
1 tablespoon gluten-free Dijon mustard
½ teaspoon onion powder
½ teaspoon garlic powder
¼ teaspoon cayenne pepper
Paprika for garnish (optional)
1 tablespoon fresh chives, finely chopped, for garnish (optional)

Preparation:

1. Place eggs in large pot with just enough water so the eggs are fully covered. (Don't fill the pot all the way.) Bring water to a boil, then turn heat off and let eggs sit in the hot water for 12 minutes (not longer).

2. Fill large bowl with ice water. Remove the eggs and place in ice water until eggs are completely cool.

3. Peel eggs, being careful not to damage the whites. Cut eggs lengthwise.

4. Gently remove the yolks without damaging the whites. If you lightly squeeze them, the yolk should pop out. Make sure you do this over a bowl.

5. Arrange egg white halves directly on a serving platter. Set aside.

6. In medium bowl, mash egg yolks, mustard, onion powder, garlic powder, cayenne, and olive oil with a fork or rubber spatula until it is smooth and creamy.

7. Use a melon scooper or a small spoon to scoop the mixture back into the egg white halves in equal amounts.

8. Sprinkle with paprika and chives, if desired. Serve immediately or refrigerate until ready to serve.

Grateful Start Grainless Maple Bread

Makes 2 small loaves

Ingredients:

½ cup almond flour

½ cup coconut flour

¼ cup golden flax meal

½ teaspoon baking soda

½ teaspoon sea salt

5 eggs

¼ cup pure maple syrup

1 teaspoon apple cider vinegar

¼ cup macadamia nut oil
  or grapeseed oil

1 tablespoon vanilla extract

Zest from one lemon, for a fresh
  citrus flavor (optional)

Preparation:

1. Preheat oven to 350°F.

2. medium bowl, mix dry ingredients: almond flour, coconut flour, flax meal, baking soda, and sea salt.

3. In large bowl, whisk eggs, maple syrup, and apple cider vinegar together. Add oil, vanilla, and lemon zest (if desired) and blend well.

4. Add dry ingredients to large bowl of wet ingredients. Mix thoroughly.

5. Pour mixture into two well-greased mini-loaf pans. Grainless breads often bake better in mini-loaf pans. You may line the pans with parchment paper if you wish to save cleanup time.

6. Place loaf pans in oven and bake for 25 to 30 minutes until toothpick inserted into center of loaf comes out clean.

7. Cool and serve.

Mood-Boosting Hummus

Serves 12

Ingredients:

2 cups garbanzo beans, soaked and cooked

4-6 garlic cloves (according to taste)

2 tablespoons tahini paste

2-3 tablespoons extra-virgin olive oil

¼ cup lemon juice

½ teaspoon paprika for garnish

¼ teaspoon sea salt

Preparation:

1. In a food processor, combine beans, garlic, tahini, and olive oil. Blend until smooth.

2. Add lemon juice and sea salt. Process until mixture is completely smooth and creamy. If mixture seems too thick, add a little more olive oil, 1 teaspoon at a time, until hummus reaches desired consistency.

3. Transfer to a serving bowl and lightly garnish with paprika.

Pleasing Pumpkin and Herb Biscuits

Serves 8

Ingredients:

½ cup organic cooked pumpkin,
   canned is fine

2 tablespoons light coconut milk

2 tablespoons honey (optional)

3 eggs

¼ cup melted coconut oil

½ teaspoon fresh rosemary, chopped

½ teaspoon fresh thyme, chopped

¾ cup almond flour

2 tablespoons coconut flour

¼ teaspoon salt (optional)

1 teaspoon baking powder

Preparation:

1. Preheat the oven to 350° F. In medium to large bowl, combine the pumpkin, coconut milk, honey, eggs, melted coconut oil, and herbs. Mix thoroughly.

2. In separate small bowl, combine almond flour, coconut flour, salt, and baking powder. Mix thoroughly.

3. Add dry ingredients to the bowl of wet ingredients and stir until mixed.

4. Line a baking sheet with parchment paper. Portion the dough with an ice cream scoop (or make them cookie size) and place onto baking sheet. Bake for 20 to 30 minutes for biscuits or about 11 to 15 minutes for cookies, depending on the portion size, until lightly browned and firm.

Roasted Broccoli Pesto Style

Serves 4

Ingredients:

1 pound broccoli, rinsed and dried

2½ tablespoons (melted but not hot) coconut oil

3-4 garlic cloves, minced

2 tablespoons chopped basil

1 teaspoon sea salt

½ teaspoon fresh ground pepper

2 teaspoons melted ghee (optional)

¼ cup roasted pine nuts (optional)

Preparation:

1. Cut broccoli into bite-sized pieces.

2. Put the broccoli in a sealable plastic bag.

3. Add coconut oil, garlic, salt, and pepper to broccoli in plastic bag. Seal and toss.

4. After broccoli is coated with seasonings, add chopped basil to bag. Seal and toss.

5. Place broccoli on coconut-oiled cookie sheet.

6. Roast at 400° F for 20 to 25 minutes until lightly browned.

7. Optional: Lightly drizzle roasted broccoli with melted ghee and top with warm roasted pine nuts.

Sprightly Mind Sautéed Spinach

Serves 4

Ingredients:

2 pounds fresh spinach

4 tablespoons pine nuts

2 tablespoons grapeseed oil

2 garlic cloves, minced

1 small onion, peeled and
   finely chopped

Pepper to taste

½ teaspoon sea salt or to taste
   (optional)

Preparation:

1. Fill bottom of large pot with water and place a steamer basket in pot. Make sure water doesn't cover the bottom of the basket. Bring water to a boil.

2. Place spinach in steamer basket and cover. Steam until spinach is wilted, about 3 to 5 minutes. Remove from heat and set aside.

3. Heat oil in large skillet over medium heat. Add garlic and onion and sauté for 3 minutes.

4. Add spinach and pine nuts. Mix well, distributing onions, garlic, and pine nuts evenly through the spinach. Heat through and remove from heat.

5. Add pepper and sea salt if desired.

Sensible Sweet Potato Mash

People often ask why sweet potatoes are so healthy if white potatoes are not. Did you know that sweet potatoes are not really related to potatoes? They are related to the morning glory flower. Unlike white potatoes, they raise blood sugar slowly. Sweet potatoes are rich in beta carotene, vitamin A, vitamin C, and many minerals. An organic sweet potato with the skin on contains more fiber than a bowl of oatmeal! These tasty root veggies are a favorite in the Amen household.

Serves 4

Ingredients:

2 sweet potatoes, peeled and diced

½ cup coconut milk

¼ teaspoon nutmeg

½ teaspoon cinnamon

Preparation:

1. Boil sweet potatoes in a large pot of water until tender, 20 minutes or so.

2. Drain sweet potatoes and transfer to large bowl or food processor.

3. Blend sweet potatoes with coconut milk, nutmeg, and cinnamon.

4. Blend until potatoes are desired consistency. Serve warm.

Wholly Guacamole

Serves 8

Ingredients:

2 ripe avocados, peeled and pitted

¼ cup red onion, peeled and finely chopped

2 tablespoons fresh chopped cilantro

1 tablespoon fresh lime juice

½ ripe tomato, seeded and diced

½ teaspoon sea salt (optional)

Preparation:

1. In medium bowl, mash avocado with a fork until smooth. (Some chunks are fine if you like chunky guacamole.)

2. Add remaining ingredients and mix well. Serve cold. Serving size: about ¼ cup

Note: Do not add tomatoes if you are not serving guacamole right away. Refrigerate guacamole without tomatoes and add them just before serving. Tomatoes will release water and make the guacamole wet.

SAUCES
AND
TOPPINGS

Blissful State Chocolate Sauce

Ingredients:

1 cup raw cacao powder

1 cup unsweetened almond milk

2 tablespoons pure maple syrup

1 dropper full of chocolate-flavored liquid stevia

½ teaspoon pure vanilla extract

2 tablespoons coconut oil

½ teaspoon cinnamon

Preparation:

1. Place all ingredients in a high-powered blender bowl. Blend until smooth and creamy.

2. Add more almond milk if necessary to achieve desired thickness. Blend well.

Suggestion: Pour sauce into a squeeze bottle for serving. For storage, pour into an airtight container and refrigerate.

Creamy Coconut Frosting

Yields a little more than 1 cup

This recipe calls for the meat from one or two young Thai coconuts. Some people are intimidated by the idea of opening coconuts to get the meat (I used to be one of them). I assure you, it is easier than it sounds, and well worth the minimal effort! The fresh coconut water and delicious meat are amazing treats. The only thing you need is a meat cleaver or a 10-inch heavy kitchen knife to get started. Young Thai coconuts can be found at Asian markets or health food stores and come wrapped in plastic. You can use other types of coconut, but the meat is often not as soft. The meat from a young Thai coconut is usually very soft, similar to the consistency of tofu.

Ingredients:

1 cup fresh coconut meat from young Thai coconuts

2-3 tablespoons raw honey (or use Sweet Leaf brand vanilla- or chocolate-flavored liquid stevia in place of honey)

¼-½ cup full-fat coconut milk

For chocolate flavor (optional):

1-2 tablespoons raw cacao powder

½ cup sugar-free chocolate chips (Lily's brand)

Preparation:

1. For chocolate flavor: Use double boiler or small saucepan and stainless steel bowl (make sure mouth of bowl is wider than mouth of the saucepan). Place chocolate chips in bowl. Boil 2 cups of water in small saucepan. Place stainless steel bowl in the boiling water and turn heat down to medium low. Melt chocolate slowly on low heat until completely soft and creamy.

2. In a high-powered blender, place meat from coconut and honey or stevia. Add ¼ cup coconut milk.

3. Turn blender on low to start. Slowly add more coconut milk as necessary to get mixture to blend. Add as little liquid as possible to keep the frosting thick, but enough to help it blend into a creamy texture. Note: If the mixture is too thick and not spreadable you may want to mix it in the food processor first, then transfer it to the blender once it is chopped. A high-powered blender will create a creamier frosting than a food processor.

Opening a Coconut:

1. Leaving the plastic wrap on the coconut, stabilize coconut on its side, pointed end sideways (over a cutting board or towel).

2. Using a 10-inch heavy kitchen knife, cut through white husk down to the coconut core, right at the edge where the coconut base goes from being a round cylinder to a point. Try not to cut through the coconut core, just down to it. It should take three or four turns of the coconut to get the entire pointy edge off.

3. Turn the coconut onto its flat base. Carefully push the tip of the knife into the exposed coconut core so that it is horizontal to the floor. The tip should easily go in at least an inch or more.

4. Firmly grasp the knife handle and carefully turn it up and away from you. The top of the coconut should pop off like a pop top.

5. Drain the delicious coconut water through a strainer into a pitcher or jar and refrigerate for drinking or using in smoothies.

6. Using a large spoon, scrape out the coconut meat.

Distinctive Onion Dill Ranch Dressing

Serves 25 (Serving size = 1 tablespoon)

Ingredients:

2 cups vegan, gluten-free mayonnaise (veganaise)

1 teaspoon garlic powder

2-3 teaspoons onion powder

1 tablespoon red wine vinegar

1-2 teaspoons fresh minced chives

1-2 teaspoons fresh chopped dill

Preparation:

1. Mix all ingredients together and serve with crudités, salad, chicken wings, or wraps. Enjoy!

Rapturous Coconut Whipped Cream

Ingredients:

2 cans full-fat coconut milk, refrigerated

2 droppers full of stevia (optional)

Preparation:

1. Refrigerate 2 cans of full-fat coconut milk overnight so the fat separates from the water.

2. Spoon coconut fat into cold bowl (refrigerate bowl if possible), being careful not to get the water in with the solids. Add stevia if desired.

3. If you have a stand mixer, start on low setting, increasing every few minutes until it's on high setting. Mix coconut fat until it reaches whipped cream consistency (can take 15 to 20 minutes).

4. Keep refrigerated until ready to serve.

Note: If you don't have a stand mixer, you can use a handheld electric mixer, but it takes patience.

Raw Chipotle Nut "Cheese"

Makes 1 cup (Serving size 1 tablespoon)

Ingredients:

2 cups pine nuts

1 large Roma tomato

1 dried chipotle pepper

2 garlic cloves

1 teaspoon sea salt

½-¾ cups purified water

1½-2 teaspoons chili powder

Juice from 1 lemon
   (about 2 tablespoons)

Optional Ingredients and Preparation: For spicier cheese, add ½ teaspoon cayenne pepper and another ½ chipotle pepper. To create a "cheese sauce," thin the mixture by adding a little more purified water and ¼ more tomato.

Preparation:

1. In a high-powered blender, combine all ingredients and blend until rich and creamy. Store in refrigerator.

2. Start with the minimum suggested ingredient amounts. Taste test before adding more. Add more water, chili powder, and chipotle pepper as desired.

Simple and Delicious Pesto Sauce

This sauce is great with Zoodles, shrimp, or eggs and can also be served over vegetables (broccoli and cauliflower).

Ingredients:

1 bunch cilantro

½ cup macadamia nuts or cashews for a fresh twist (or pine nuts for traditional taste)

2 cloves garlic

¼ teaspoon sea salt

½ cup macadamia nut oil

Preparation:

1. Blend all ingredients in a food processor until smooth.

2. Use according to recipe needs or store in airtight container and refrigerate for future use. Sauce can hold for up to two weeks.

Zesty Aioli Sauce

Serves 4

Ingredients:

¼ cup veganaise

¼ cup sugar-free ketchup
   (Nature's Hollow brand)

¼ teaspoon onion powder

¼ teaspoon garlic powder

¼ teaspoon sea salt

¼-½ teaspoon chili powder
   (I prefer ancho chili powder)

Preparation:

1. Whisk all ingredients together in small bowl until smooth and creamy.

2. Divide mixture evenly into four small sauce cups or store in an airtight container and refrigerate for future use. Sauce will last about seven to 10 days.

SNACKS

Coco Banana Delight

Serves 1

Ingredients:

¼ banana

1-2 tablespoons almond butter

1 Paleo Wrap

Preparation:

1. Spread almond butter on wrap.

2. Cut banana into small bite-size pieces and put on wrap.

3. Roll wrap with almond butter and banana inside.

Festive Frozen Grapes

Frozen grapes make a great snack and are fun substitutes for ice cubes in water.

Ingredients:

1 bunch red or black grapes

1 bunch green grapes

Preparation:

1. Wash bunches of red or black and green grapes.

2. Cut grapes into small clusters. Pat dry and place on a tray or in a bowl. Allow to freeze for at least two hours.

Astute Apple Sandwich

Serves 2

These simple treats are an amazing afternoon snack for homework or play dates. They will help keep distracted, active kids focused and happy, without the chemicals and sugar of processed foods.

Ingredients:

1 large apple, sliced into rings or wedges

2 tablespoons almond butter, cashew butter, or sunflower seed butter

1 tablespoon cacao nibs, coconut flakes, or granola crumble (optional)

Preparation:

1. Line dish or platter with ½ of the apple rings or wedges.

2. Evenly spread the nut or seed butter between them.

3. Sprinkle with the topping of your choice.

4. Place remaining apple slices or wedges on top of lower halves. Voila! Sandwiches are ready to serve.

Go-Well Trail Mix

Serves 6

Ingredients:

¼ cup raw cashews

¼ cup raw slivered almonds

¼ cup raw walnuts

¼ cup halved pecans

¼ cup chopped macadamia nuts

¼ cup raw cacao nibs

2 tablespoons goji berries, unsweetened

2 tablespoons golden berries or golden raisins

2 tablespoons shaved coconut, unsweetened

¼ cup sugar-free dark chocolate chips (Lily's Brand)

Preparation:

1. Mix all ingredients well and store in an airtight container until ready to use.

Keen Garlic Kale Chips

Serves 4

Ingredients:

1 bunch organic curly-leaf kale, leaves torn from stems into large bite-sized pieces

2 tablespoons grapeseed or macadamia nut oil

2 tablespoons ghee or coconut oil

2 garlic cloves, minced

¼ teaspoon garlic powder

Sea salt to taste

Optional ingredients:
   Try this with your favorite spices (curry and onion powder make a great alternative)

Preparation:

1. Preheat oven to 350° F. Line a baking sheet with parchment paper and set aside.

2. Place grapeseed or macadamia nut oil, ghee, garlic, and garlic powder in a saucepan over low heat for 2 to 3 minutes. Remove from heat and let cool for about 10 to 12 minutes.

3. Lay kale on cutting board or in large bowl and drizzle topping over leaves. Use your hands to be sure that the kale leaves are completely covered with topping (rub it in gently).

4. Spread kale leaves out on baking sheet.

5. Bake for about 15 minutes, turning leaves once and rotating baking sheet. Watch carefully for the last few minutes. If kale looks like it is starting to brown, remove immediately.

6. Salt according to taste. Enjoy!

Omni Grainless Granola Protein Bars

These delicious bars can be made in advance and hold up well when stored in the refrigerator.

Serves 12

Ingredients:

2 tablespoons cacao butter (coconut oil is not a good substitute)

½ cup raw pumpkin seeds

½ cup walnuts or cashews

½ cup shredded raw, unsweetened coconut

½ cup almond meal

¼ cup chocolate-flavored protein powder (pea protein, sweetened with stevia; I use Omni Protein by BrainMD at BrainMD.com)

½ cup raw sunflower seeds

1 teaspoon cinnamon

¼ teaspoon cloves

½ teaspoon ginger

1 teaspoon vanilla extract

2 tablespoons macadamia nut oil

¼ cup organic honey

⅛ cup monk fruit

2 tablespoons sugar-free dark chocolate chips (Lily's brand)

2 tablespoons dried goji berries or mulberries

Coconut oil or grapeseed oil for greasing pan

Preparation:

1. Preheat oven to 350° F.

2. In small saucepan, melt cacao butter over low heat. Note: Bars will not hold together without the cacao butter. Coconut oil is not a good substitute.

3. Using a food processor, grind pumpkin seeds, nuts, and coconut until you achieve the texture of coarse flour. Place mixture in large bowl.

4. Mix in almond meal, protein powder, sunflower seeds, cinnamon, cloves, and ginger. The mixture will be thick, so you may need to use your hands to mix it thoroughly.

5. Add vanilla, macadamia nut oil, and cacao butter. Mix well with a fork or rubber spatula.

6. Add honey and monk fruit and mix well.

7. Fold in chips and berries and mix well.

8. Lightly grease 9 x 9-inch baking pan with coconut oil or grapeseed oil (or use a nonstick baking pan). Press mixture into the pan until it is even on all sides. Bake for 10 to 15 minutes or until lightly golden.

9. Refrigerate for 30 minutes, then take mixture out and bring to room temperature. This allows the cacao butter to harden again so bars will hold together.

10. Remove from baking pan and cut into 12 bars

Pumpkin Protein Bars

Serves approximately 12

Ingredients:

1 15-ounce can organic pumpkin

¼ cup light coconut milk

2 tablespoons macadamia nut oil

1 teaspoon vanilla extract

5 egg whites

¼ cup raw honey

⅓ cup monk fruit

¾ cup almond meal

¾ cup all-purpose gluten-free flour

¼ flax meal

¼ cup vanilla-flavored protein powder (pea protein, sweetened with stevia; I use Omni Protein by BrainMD at BrainMD.com)

2 teaspoons baking powder

1 teaspoon baking soda

1 tablespoon pumpkin pie spice

Creamy Coconut Frosting (see recipe in Sauces and Toppings)

Preparation:

1. Preheat oven to 350˚ F.

2. Using a handheld electric mixer at medium speed, beat together the pumpkin, coconut milk, oil, vanilla, egg whites, honey, and monk fruit until smooth.

3. In separate bowl, mix dry ingredients: almond meal, flour, flax meal, protein powder, baking powder, baking soda, and pumpkin pie spice.

4. Combine dry ingredients with wet ingredients. Using the electric mixer, mix on medium to high speed until the batter is thoroughly combined and smooth.

5. Spray a jellyroll (10½ x 15) baking pan with nonstick cooking spray and spread batter evenly into pan. Bake for 20 to 25 minutes. Let cool completely before frosting then cut into 12 bars.

Note: If you decide not to use frosting, you can add ½ cup sugar-free dark chocolate chips to batter. Reserve a few chips to scatter over the top.

Stay Sharp Pizza Snacks — Two Ways

This snack is a great alternative to high-carb snacks before homework. Since pizza is a general favorite, it's a great "gateway" into getting kids to eat healthy. There are two versions of this snack. One version is made with zucchini or squash, and most kids love it! The second version may be made with gluten-free bread or pre-made gluten-free pizza dough that can be kept in the freezer. Although I don't use this often, I have found it to be a quick and fun after-school snack for play dates when I don't want to be the "weird" mom that is always serving "green" stuff. It can be a great intro to healthy food for some of the neighborhood kids.

Sauce Ingredients:

1 large jar organic marinara sauce or pizza sauce (I prefer garlic and herb flavor and recommend using a sugar-free product.) If you prefer to make the sauce from scratch, the ingredients are as follows:

¼ cup olive oil

1 onion, peeled and diced

2 garlic cloves, minced

¼ cup finely chopped parsley

1 28-ounce can sugar-free diced tomatoes

1 28-ounce can sugar-free tomato sauce

2 4-ounce cans tomato paste

1 teaspoon dried oregano or 1 tablespoon fresh, chopped

1 teaspoon dried basil or 1 tablespoon fresh, chopped

1 teaspoon sea salt

Preparation:

1. Heat oil in large pot over medium heat. Add onion and sauté for about 3 minutes.

2. Add garlic and sauté for another 2 minutes.

3. Stir in remaining ingredients. Reduce heat to low and simmer for 20 to 30 minutes.

Pizza Base Option 1

Ingredients:

2 large zucchini, cut in half horizontally

Pizza Base Option 2

Ingredients:

Gluten-free bread or pizza dough (Whole Foods makes a great pre-made gluten-free dough)

Preparation:

1. Preheat oven or toaster oven to 400° F. (I like the toaster oven for these simple snacks.) Roll out dough.

2. If you are using gluten-free bread, lightly toast the bread first to prevent it from getting too soggy.

3. Spread a thin layer of sauce on base of your choice (zucchini, gluten-free bread, or pizza crust).

4. Add dairy-free cheese if desired and other toppings of your choice.

5. Place pizza snacks on parchment lined cookie sheet and bake for about 15 to 20 minutes (bread may take less time). Zucchini takes longer than the bread, so make sure the zucchini is soft.

6. If serving to children, allow the sauce to cool a bit before serving.

Optional toppings:

Daiya dairy-free cheese

Sun-dried tomatoes

Ground turkey or beef

Uncured pepperoni

Lunch meat without nitrates

Olives

Onions

Pineapple

Ham

Temper Me Sweet Potato Chips

Serves 3-5

Ingredients:

2 tablespoons grapeseed or macadamia nut oil

1 organic sweet potato, skin on

⅛ teaspoon sea salt

Pepper to taste (optional)

Preparation:

1. Preheat oven to 400˚ F.

2. Lightly brush a baking sheet with 1 teaspoon of oil. Set baking sheet aside.

3. Cut sweet potato into very thin slices. A mandolin works very well for this.

4. Arrange potato slices on the baking sheet in a single layer.

5. Using a brush, lightly coat potato slices with oil, top side only.

6. Bake for about 10 minutes, then rotate the pan. Bake for another 10 minutes or until sweet potatoes are golden crisp around edges.

7. Remove tray from the oven and sprinkle with salt and pepper as desired.

Smoked Salmon Boats

Serves 4

Ingredients:

1 bunch baby asparagus (trim tough ends and make the stalks short enough to fit into the endive)

1 teaspoon grapeseed oil

1 teaspoon fresh oregano

8 ounces wild smoked salmon, cut into 2-ounce strips

8 endive leaves

Preparation:

1. Boil a small amount of purified water in the bottom of a large pot. Place a steamer basket in the bottom of the pot and be sure the water does not cover the bottom of the basket.

2. Steam asparagus in the boiling water until tender but not mushy, about 10 minutes. Sprinkle oregano over asparagus for the final 3 minutes of cooking.

3. Remove asparagus from steamer basket and be sure it is completely dry of excess water.

4. Arrange endive leaves on a platter.

5. Place strips of salmon lengthwise on each endive leaf.

6. Add several asparagus stalks over each strip of salmon and serve.

DESSERTS

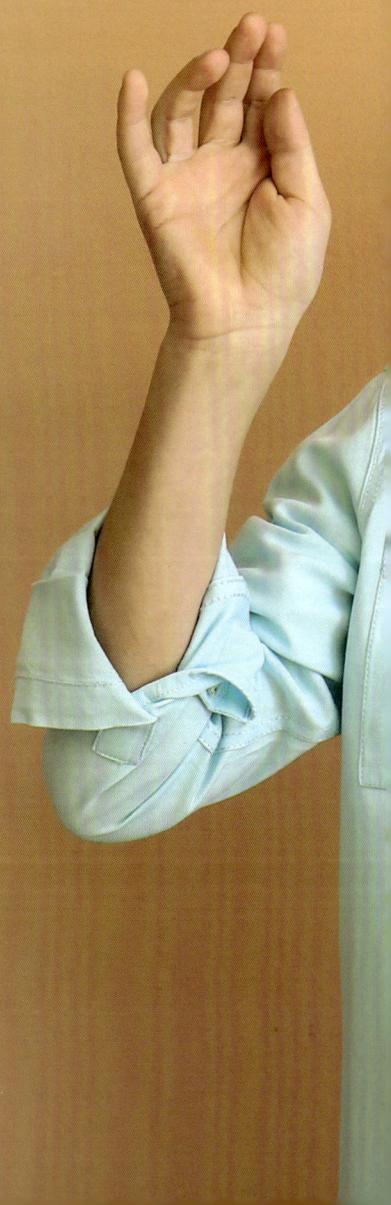

Chloe's Party Root Beer Float

This simple recipe is always a hit with our daughter's friends at birthday parties and special occasions. It contains about 10 percent of the sugar of a traditional root beer float and it's dairy and gluten free.

Serves 1

Ingredients:

1 can root beer-flavored Zevia

¼ cup vanilla-flavored sugar- and gluten-free coconut milk ice cream

Preparation:

1. Pour contents of can into a tall glass and add ice cream. Serve immediately.

Chilled Coco Elation Bites

Serves 16 or more

Ingredients:

1 cup coconut oil (softened)

¼ cup almond butter

1-2 tablespoons pure maple syrup (it tastes great without much sweetener)

½ teaspoon vanilla extract

Pinch of salt (optional)

1 ounce sugar-free chocolate, shaved or finely chopped, or 2 tablespoons sugar-free dark chocolate chips (BrainMD's Brain in Love or Lily's Brand)

16-20 paper candy or truffle cups (optional)

Preparation:

1. Line baking sheet with individual paper candy paper cups. If you don't want to use candy cups, line a 9 x 9-inch baking sheet with parchment paper and make a single sheet instead (breaking it into pieces of "bark").

2. In a blender, place all ingredients except shaved chocolate. Blend until smooth and creamy. You may mix ingredients in a bowl with a rubber spatula, but the blender gets the lumps out of the coconut oil and almond butter. Transfer mixture to medium bowl.

3. Using a teaspoon, spoon the mixture into the candy cups.

4. Using a teaspoon, sprinkle the top with shaved chocolate, or place a chocolate chip on top of each cup instead. If you are not using candy cups, pour the mixture onto the parchment-lined cookie sheet.

5. Place the baking sheet in the freezer for at least 30 minutes or until the pieces solidify.

6. Serve in individual candy cups or break up the sheet into bark and share (don't worry about making pieces uniform size and shape).

Choco-tentment Mousse

See notes on working with Thai coconuts in the Creamy Coconut Frosting recipe

Serves 4

Ingredients:

Coconut meat from one or two fresh young Thai coconuts (about 1 cup)

2-3 tablespoons full-fat coconut milk (refrigerate the can for several hours)

1-2 tablespoon raw cacao powder (start with 1 tablespoon)

½ cup coconut butter or raw almond butter

1 tablespoon coconut oil

½ teaspoon vanilla extract

½ teaspoon cinnamon

2 tablespoons pure maple syrup or raw honey

Optional Ingredients:

10-12 drops stevia liquid sweetener (chocolate flavor, Sweet Leaf brand)

1 cup fresh berries of your choice (I love raspberries or sliced strawberries)

Rapturous Coconut Whipped Cream (see recipe in Sauces and Toppings)

Preparations:

1. Blend all ingredients except berries in a high-powered blender.

2. If desired, place berries in bottom of dessert cup.

3. Layer mixture over berries into dessert bowls and refrigerate for 30 minutes before serving.

4. Top with coconut whipped cream if desired.

Omni Apple Crisp Squares

I like to use red apples for this recipe or a combination of red and green.

Serves 16

Filling Ingredients:

7 apples, peeled and chopped
   (Try using the slicer attachment
   on a food processor as a shortcut.)

1 teaspoon cinnamon

½ teaspoon nutmeg

¼ teaspoon ginger

½ tablespoon grapeseed oil
   (for greasing pan)

⅓ cup monk fruit (optional)

Crumble Topping Ingredients:

¼ cup pecans or walnuts

¼ cup almond flour

2 tablespoons unsweetened
   almond butter

6 dates

Preparation:

1. Preheat oven to 350° F.

2. Place apples in medium pan over medium heat. Apples will release fluid and begin to dehydrate after a couple of minutes. Add cinnamon, nutmeg, ginger, and monk fruit, if desired. Cook until apples are hot and soft, about 15 minutes. Don't allow apples to dry out and burn.

3. Remove apples from heat and pour into a 9 x 9-inch greased baking dish.

4. Mix all topping ingredients in food processor until well blended and chunky.

5. Remove crumble topping from food processor and sprinkle on top of the apples in baking dish. Bake the apple crisp for 15 minutes.

6. Use an ice cream scoop to spoon small portions into dessert bowls. Serve warm or cold.

Chunky Monkey Frozen Bananas

Serves 4

Frozen Banana Ingredients:

½ cup chocolate sauce

2 slightly green bananas, peeled

¼ cup finely chopped cashews
   or ¼ cup shredded coconut

4 Popsicle sticks

Chocolate Sauce Ingredients:

1 cup raw cacao powder

1 cup unsweetened almond milk

4 tablespoons pure maple syrup

1 dropper full of chocolate-flavored liquid stevia

½ teaspoon pure vanilla extract

2 tablespoons coconut oil

½ teaspoon cinnamon

Preparation:

1. Place all Chocolate Sauce ingredients in a high-powered blender bowl. Blend until smooth and creamy.

2. Pour chocolate sauce into a wide saucer or dinner plate so it's easy to dip and roll the bananas.

3. Put nuts or coconut in another wide saucer or dinner plate.

4. Cover a small tray with wax paper.

5. Cut bananas in half crosswise and insert Popsicle sticks in cut end of each banana.

6. Holding the stick, dip each banana into the chocolate sauce, rolling and coating the entire banana.

7. Immediately dip the bananas in the nuts or coconut, rolling to coat.

8. Lay coated bananas on wax paper and place tray in freezer for at least 20 minutes to allow chocolate to set.

9. Refrigerate leftover sauce in airtight container for later use. Sauce will store for over a week.

Omni Blueberry Cobbler

Serves 8

Blueberry Filling Ingredients:

6 cups organic blueberries

1 teaspoon vanilla extract

1 teaspoon arrowroot

1 ½ tablespoons monk fruit
(use a little more if berries are bitter)
or 2 tablespoons honey

Crust Ingredients:

1 teaspoon ghee or coconut oil
for greasing pan

½ cup all-purpose gluten-free flour
or brown rice flour

½ cup almond meal

1 teaspoon baking powder

⅓ cup monk fruit

2 tablespoons melted ghee or
Earth Balance Butter replacement
(soy free)

½-1 cup almond milk, unsweetened

1 teaspoon cinnamon

1 tablespoon monk fruit for sprinkle

Preparation:

1. Preheat oven to 375˚ F.

2. Grease 9 x 9-inch baking dish
with ghee or coconut oil.

3. Place blueberries in baking dish. Toss vanilla, arrowroot, and monk fruit (or drizzle honey over the top) with berries.

4. In medium bowl, combine all-purpose flour or brown rice flour, almond meal, baking powder, ghee or Earth Balance Butter, and monk fruit.

5. Slowly mix in just enough milk to make mixture a thick batter, not runny (only ½ cup to start). Add more as necessary.

6. Spoon batter over berries leaving a few small gaps for the berries to show through. Mix cinnamon and monk fruit in a spice jar and set aside.

7. Bake cobbler for 45 minutes or until the top is golden brown.

8. Sprinkle the cinnamon and monk fruit mixture over the top. Serve warm in dessert cups.

Creamy Coco-Mint Melts

Serves 16-20

Ingredients:

½ cup coconut oil

½ cup coconut butter, softened

2 teaspoons mint extract

10 drops chocolate-flavored liquid stevia (Sweet Leaf brand)

1 tablespoon wild honey or pure maple syrup (optional)

2 teaspoons finely chopped fresh mint

2 teaspoons sugar-free shaved chocolate (Lily's Brand or BrainMD's Brain on Joy)

16-20 truffle candy paper cups (for freezing)

Preparation:

1. In a high-powered blender (or in medium bowl with rubber spatula), blend coconut oil, coconut butter, mint extract, stevia, and honey or syrup (if desired) until smooth and creamy. Blending in a high-powered blender will get the lumps out of the coconut butter.

2. Pour mixture into medium bowl. Fold in chopped mint and mix well. If you mix mint in the blender, the mixture will turn green.

3. Line up truffle candy cups on a baking sheet and spoon a small amount of mixture into each cup.

4. Using a teaspoon, lightly dust the top of each candy cup with shaved chocolate.

5. Place baking sheet in freezer on a flat surface for at least 30 minutes Serve cold.

Orange Creamsicle Bar

Freeze time: 4 hours

Ingredients:

3-4 peeled, seedless oranges

½-1 cup light coconut milk

½ teaspoon vanilla extract

10 drops orange-flavored liquid stevia (Sweet Leaf brand) (optional)

½ cup sugar-free dark chocolate chips (Lily's brand) (optional)

Preparation:

1. In a blender, blend oranges, coconut milk, vanilla, and stevia (if desired) until smooth and creamy. Add more coconut milk for creamier texture.

2. Add chocolate chips (if desired) and blend for a few seconds more. Do not over blend the chips. You want them to be in small bits, not completely blended in.

3. Pour mixture into popsicle trays and freeze for 3 to 4 hours until frozen solid.

4. Allow Creamsicles to thaw for about 5 minutes before trying to remove them from the tray.

Note: You can also make Creamsicles with pineapple, watermelon, or strawberries.

Tropical Frozen Treats

Freeze time: 4 hours

Ingredients:

2-3 organic strawberries, sliced

½ cup organic frozen blueberries

4-6 frozen peach or mango slices

4-8 kiwi slices, frozen or fresh

1 to 1½ cups coconut water

Preparation:

1. Divide strawberries, blueberries, peaches or mangoes, and kiwi evenly among four Popsicle trays. Place the fruit in the trays in alternating order, filling the trays but not damaging the fruit. (Don't try to smash the fruit pieces together; allow them to gently rest upon one another.)

2. When all trays have been filled with the fruit, pour coconut water over fruit, filling trays to the top.

3. Freeze for 3 to 4 hours until frozen solid.

4. Allow frozen treats to thaw for about 5 minutes before trying to remove them from the tray.

Nutty Butter Cups

Serves 12

Ingredients:

8 ounces dark chocolate, sugar free and dairy free

¼ cup almond butter or seed butter (no stir)

2 tablespoons coconut oil (optional)

Preparation:

1. Line a mini-muffin pan with candy paper or mini-muffin liners. Standard muffin liners will be too large.

2. In a microwave-safe bowl, put about 2 ½ ounces of the chocolate and coconut oil if desired. If using chocolate bars, break into pieces. Coconut oil is not necessary, but it will give you a bit of grace, guaranteeing you don't burn your chocolate, and that you get smooth, creamy sauce every time. Heat chocolate in 20- to 30-second intervals, stirring each time. Heat until the chocolate is completely melted and smooth, being careful not to burn it. If you prefer heating chocolate over the stove, either heat over low heat using a double boiler or use a small pot and stir constantly so the chocolate doesn't burn.

3. When chocolate is liquefied, spoon about ½ teaspoon of the chocolate mix into each candy paper, just enough to cover the bottom of the paper.

4. Put tray in the freezer for about 5 minutes so chocolate hardens. While chocolate is cooling in the freezer, melt remaining chocolate and coconut oil (if desired).

5. Remove tray from freezer. Drop teaspoon–size balls of nut butter in the middle of each cup, on top of the hardened chocolate base. Press lightly to flatten the ball so that the nut butter doesn't protrude over the top of the cup, but don't smash it down. The nut butter should remain in the center and not bleed out the edges of the chocolate base.

6. Spoon remaining chocolate mixture into each cup, covering the nut butter completely. Be sure to get the sauce around the sides. If necessary, flatten the top and smooth over with chocolate. If chocolate doesn't surround the sides of the nut butter, the nut butter will show through, and the cups will fall apart.

7. Freeze for about 15 minutes before serving.